THE
EGOTISTICAL SUBLIME

THE EGOTISTICAL SUBLIME

A History of WORDSWORTH'S IMAGINATION

By

JOHN JONES

Fellow of Merton College
Oxford

1970

CHATTO & WINDUS

LONDON

Published by
Chatto and Windus Ltd
London

*   .

Clarke, Irwin and Co. Ltd
Toronto

ISBN 0 7011 0861 4

First Published 1954
Second Impression 1960
This Edition 1964
Second Impression 1970

Printed in Great Britain by
Lewis Reprints Limited, Port Talbot,
Glamorgan

For William Bell
1924-1948

NOTE

I refer to *Wordsworth's Poetical Works*, edited by Professor Ernest de Selincourt and Dr Helen Darbishire, in the case of texts and variants of texts that will not be found in the Oxford Standard Authors Edition. References to *The Prelude* are, unless otherwise stated, to the text of 1805, which is published in a separate volume of the Oxford Standard Authors.

PREFACE

THIS is a book of some pretension in its attempt to minister to truths that lie too often unregarded, bedridden in an outhouse of the soul.

The work of the Romantics, poets and novelists, celebrates the fact of love, at once marvellously evident and difficult beyond despair, and about which the age immediately preceding them had been less than honest. This is true also of Wordsworth's poetry, but in so peculiar a sense as to make us wonder how he can be called Romantic; for he begins with a vision of Sympathy that belongs, in so far as genius can belong anywhere, to the eighteenth century, and he ends with the Religion of Gratitude, tractarian and catholic in its associations.

While discussing these things I refer frequently to Coleridge, in the belief that his history and Wordsworth's continue to illuminate each other, by way of contrast, throughout their lives; and although I essay greater intellectual rigour than is usually thought necessary for interpretative criticism, I do so in the name of literature and not of philosophy. If, as seems the case with all philosophical thinking below the highest level of European achievement, clarity can be gained only at the cost of imaginative faintness, then we must persevere within that warm chaos which is critical tradition and in which the idea of poetry can be at least entertained. Even third-rate critics have touched a relevant humility and wonder.

An argument may be unphilosophical, arbitrary in its choice of route and its crossing of categorical frontiers, yet it need not be without its own kind of discipline. If there is no structural method, the way into the critical activity is unimportant. Thus Words-

worth made two suggestions to Coleridge for his
Ancient Mariner. One of these was the albatross, the
lonely bird which I relate to Wordsworth's preoccupation with solitude. The other was the navigation
of the ship by the dead men. Of this I make no use at
all, but only through an accident of inclination; for the
two poets might well be approached by way of their
attitudes to death. In early versions of the Immortality
Ode the child thinks of the grave, without horror or
disgust, as

> but a lonely bed without the sense or sight
> Of day or the warm light,
> A place of thought where we in waiting lie. . . .

Coleridge called this a "frightful notion", and persuaded Wordsworth to omit all reference to the child's
vision of life in death. Implicit in this clash of imaginations is a profound difference in understanding of the
life of thought and of sensation, of the Christian reality
of sin and judgment, of relationship with God and
Nature. The argument might have been quite other
than what it is, but directed towards the same conclusion.

If the study is unphilosophical, so is its subject.
Wordsworth, though no fool, was no philosopher; and
it were very perverse to seek a respectable metaphysical
home for his poetry. The most that we can say, which
may be everything or almost nothing, is that all appre-
hensions of truth support each other simply in their
humanity. Only through Wordsworth's sentiment of
the "one human heart" is it worth while to consider
his own ethical severity, his view of language as a mode
of Nature, and the commanding of expressive forms as
an exercise of practical reason pursued intuitively beyond the phenomenal limits of speculation. Only in this
spirit is his power of deep gazing upon objects to be
referred to that "change in the shading" of which

Husserl speaks, whereby a man may transform "a
pure psychology of the inner life into a self-styled
transcendental phenomenology". Thus, in striving for
final synthesis, the great movement of his life towards
solitude, then away, seems less a defeat than a discovery.
Aquinas had shown that singulars in the world are
infinite, but only potentially so. The moral may rest
here.

CONTENTS

I

THE ARGUMENT

SINCE Wordsworth died, nothing has influenced the
fortunes of his poetry so much as Matthew Arnold's
Golden Treasury Selection. Nor is this hard to understand. Arnold's is a good Selection, and the path which
he found through that vast extent of Pastoral and
Patriotism is one which later explorers, critics and
general readers alike, have been glad to follow. Also,
and again because he selected well, Arnold made it impossible for those who came after him to ignore the fact
that most of Wordsworth's best poetry was written
within the single decade preceding the publication, in
1807, of his *Poems in Two Volumes*. This, more than
anything else, has commanded the attention of writers
on Wordsworth, and has produced a mass of speculation as to the cause of his decline.

But there is another and less obvious way in which
Arnold's influence has been both widespread and enduring. He tells his readers, in the Preface to his
Selection, to forget about Wordsworth's philosophy
and to devote themselves to his poetry. Wordsworth
the philosopher, says Arnold, is a sham; but Wordsworth the poet stands next to Shakespeare and Milton.
And this judgment, apparently innocent in its Victorian
largeness, is the beginning of our troubles.

Coleridge would have disagreed with Arnold. His
knowledge of Wordsworth's poetry up to 1814—in
particular, of the unpublished *Prelude*—led him to
look forward to *The Recluse* as "the *first* and *only* true
philosophical poem in existence".[1] In 1814 *The
Excursion* was published, a poem of 10,000 lines, but
still a mere instalment of the great *Recluse*, Words-

---

[1] *Letters of S. T. Coleridge* (ed. E. H. Coleridge), Vol. II. p. 648.

worth's intended life work. In *The Excursion* Coleridge
expected to find a Christian Philosophy, and, as he
admitted quite frankly,[1] he was disappointed. Now
Arnold's attack on Wordsworth's philosophy was
aimed primarily at *The Excursion*, which suggests that
Coleridge came in the end to anticipate Arnold's view
of Wordsworth. But this is not so. Arnold's quarrel
with *The Excursion* was really a quarrel with his own
generation, with the moral enthusiasm that confuses
pietism and philosophy. *The Excursion* is certainly much
more than pietism, but it is less than Christian apolo-
getic: despite the doctrine strewn about its surface, it
contains neither sustained defence nor clear affirmation
of belief; and Arnold was not tempted by the ethical
and undogmatic nature of his own Christianity to call
The Excursion philosophical. Instead, he poked fun at
earnest Wordsworthians, and their talk of the philosopher-poet. And here Arnold and Coleridge are never
on common ground; for Coleridge continued, despite
his disappointment, to maintain that "Wordsworth
possessed more of the genius of a great philosophical
poet than any man I ever knew, or, as I believe, has
existed in England since Milton".[2] Both good critics,
Coleridge and Arnold were both traffickers in
generality. Coleridge believed that "no man was ever
yet a great poet without being at the same time a profound philosopher"[3]; and Arnold dallied to little purpose with his distinguishing of philosopher and poet.
To learn from them, we must ask direct questions.

Why did Arnold consider Wordsworth a great poet?
That he discovered in Wordsworth's poetry a searching
criticism of life, is no answer; for this was Arnold's
universal measure of greatness. He has, as it turns out,
something more to say. "In Wordsworth's case, the

---

[1] *Letters of S. T. Coleridge* (ed. E. H. Coleridge), Vol. II. pp. 645-6.
[2] *Table Talk*, July 31, 1832.
[3] *Biographia Literaria* (ed. J. Shawcross), Vol. II. p. 19.

accident, for so it may be called, of inspiration, is of peculiar importance." "He has no style." "Nature seems to take the pen out of his hand and to write for him with her own bare, sheer, penetrating power."[1] This is a graceful evasion; but not on that account to be ignored. Arnold strikes an attitude in which Words-worthian criticism has for the most part persisted—less prettily, as the years pass, and with vague gestures towards the poetry of the Great Decade.

We must ask Arnold what sort of poetry it is that Nature writes for Wordsworth.

> He laid us as we lay at birth
> On the cool flowery lap of earth.[2]

Arnold's answer amounts to this: it is redemptive poetry. Its office is to deliver us from a stale, tired, doubt-ridden world, and restore us to a world fresh and undivided. This world is recognized at once as the home of the Scholar Gipsy; and although we cannot determine its limits exactly—Arnold had no clear sight of it himself, and in any case his invocation of the Oxford countryside diverts our attention—it is certainly less Christian than Pagan: it wears not the innocence of the Garden of Eden, but the brightness, the poetic immediacy of the Golden Age.

The Scholar Gipsy learnt a secret which enabled him to escape from this world and to find another. He promised, when he left, that he would return one day and divulge his secret; but even if he had kept this promise, he could not have helped Wordsworth to write *The Recluse:* Wordsworth's task was to make sense of this world, not to find a better and a timeless one. This is clearly brought out by Coleridge when, late in life, he reverts to the scheme of *The Recluse:*

> Then the plan laid out, and, I believe, partly suggested by me, was that Wordsworth should assume the station of a man

---

[1] Preface to *Golden Treasury Selection.*   [2] *Memorial Verses.*

in mental repose, one whose principles were made up, and so prepared to deliver upon authority a system of philosophy. He was to treat man as man—a subject of eye, ear, touch, and taste, in contact with external nature, and informing the senses from the mind, and not compounding a mind out of the senses; then he was to describe the pastoral and other states of society, assuming something of the Juvenalian spirit as he approached the high civilization of cities and towns, and opening a melancholy picture of the present state of degeneracy and vice; thence he was to infer and reveal the proof of, and necessity for, the whole state of man and society being subject to, and illustrative of, a redemptive process in operation, showing how this idea reconciled all the anomalies, and promised future glory and restoration. Something of this sort was, I think, agreed on. It is, in substance, what I have been all my life doing in my system of philosophy.[1]

Unlike Arnold, Coleridge actually talks about redemption, intending that the word shall bear a Christian meaning. This brings in issue his own and Wordsworth's Christianity; and here we must be clear about dates. *The Recluse* was first thought of in the early months of 1798, at a time when Wordsworth and Coleridge were working together in close poetic partnership. Then, while the grand design was being evolved, Coleridge was still a disciple of Priestley and Frend in the Unitarian faith; his religion enthusiastic, but almost entirely innocent of doctrine. It is true that his attitude towards Wordsworth's Christianity was sometimes critical, but the criticism was aimed at his faint heart rather than his false opinions. He detected in Wordsworth a certain hesitancy, and was once or twice offended by his irreverent tone when speaking of religion.[2] Nevertheless, the measure of agreement

[1] *Table Talk*, July 31, 1832.
[2] *Letters* (ed. E. H. Coleridge), Vol. I. pp. 164, 246. *Anima Poetae* (ed. E. H. Coleridge), p. 35.

between them is of much greater importance than their differences: both, at this time, were trying to graft some sort of Christianity on to the dry and feeble stem of eighteenth-century deism; and Coleridge's account of *The Recluse*, in its confident, demonstrative tone, and its independence of revealed religion, catches the quality of this effort to study the world and to prove, as it were by internal evidence, both its need of a Redeemer and the fact of its redemption. But when he proceeds to say, of Wordsworth's aim in *The Recluse*, that "it is, in substance, what I have been all my life doing in my system of philosophy", he invites misunderstanding. Both Wordsworth and he moved a long way from the position which they held in 1798; and they did not travel together. They were in any case very different men.

Coleridge knew himself too well to suppose that he could live by philosophy alone, or yet to deny that philosophy nourished and supported him. "In certain waters," he said, "it may teach the exact depth and prevent a drowning."[1] When, in his discussion of the scheme of *The Recluse*, he speaks of the relationship between man and the external world, between the mind and the senses, we must place his remarks in the context of his reading in philosophy. Without some knowledge of philosophers there can be no understanding of Coleridge, for he lived with them and they helped to shape his world. He dealt instinctively in the currency of intellect, and the instinct was a deep one. In his own philosophizing one looks in vain for consistency of achievement; but there is a kind of consistency of intellectual effort, not to be passed over.

Coleridge wrote, in 1797: "My mind feels as if it ached to behold and know something *great*, something

[1] *Anima Poetae* (ed. E. H. Coleridge), p. 255.

one and *indivisible*. And it is only in the faith of that, that rocks or waterfalls, mountains or caverns, give me the sense of sublimity or majesty."[1] And in an autobiographical letter of the same year, he argued, in defence of his childhood reading of fairy stories and tales of adventure: "I know of no other way of giving the mind a love of the Great and the Whole."[2] The love of the great and the whole, and the struggle for its secure possession, is the story of Coleridge's life, both in thought and in art. Wherever we enter Coleridge's philosophy, we come upon Descartes' reduction of reality into the distinct kinds of thought and extension; a discovery which should not surprise us since the Cartesian Dichotomy has to a large extent determined the form of metaphysical thinking since the Renaissance. Perhaps reality is dualistic, constituted in this way of thinking things and extended things. And perhaps there can be no intercourse between the two kinds. But metaphysicians who admit the first nearly all deny the second, in the interest of knowledge and morality. They attempt to bridge the gulf between the self and the external world and thus to save philosophy; some, like Descartes himself, by means of scientific theories regarding mind and matter, and others by appealing to God as the Underwriter of appearance.

There is a second metaphysical tradition in which Descartes' initial dichotomy is denied, a tradition into which Coleridge eventually found his way. His theory of art serves to introduce us to this manner of thinking. "To make the external internal, the internal external, to make Nature thought and thought Nature—this is the mystery of genius in the Fine Arts."[3] Coleridge is on familiar ground: he is talking Idealism and

---

[1] *Letters* (ed. E. H. Coleridge), Vol. I. p. 228.

[2] *Ibid.*, p. 16.

[3] "Essay on Poesy or Art", *Biographia Literaria* (ed. J. Shawcross), Vol. II. p. 258.

he is heavily in debt to a German—in this case to Schelling.

The language of Idealism came naturally to Coleridge. He remained, throughout all his philosophical wanderings, a Platonist, and he saw the post-Kantian movement in which he took part as a return to Greek modes of thought. His own philosophy is dominated by the organic metaphor and by the dialectical method, and it can lay claim to more originality than Coleridge, by his widespread and usually unacknowledged borrowings, has led people to believe. The dialectic is itself in point. Coleridge is often assumed to be echoing Hegel; but this cannot be so, for he knew no Hegel when he evolved his own method, the true ancestry of which may be discovered in the references, scattered throughout his writings, to Heraclitus and his philosophy of flux, to Bruno's Polar Principle, and, more immediately, to the triadic form in which Kant disposed his categories, described by Coleridge as "the prominent excellence in Kant's *Critique of the Pure Reason*".[1] The weakness of his philosophy is not that it is derivative, but that it seeks to be Christian. He fails to perform the first, in a sense the impossible, task of Christian philosophy, which is to reconcile Greek thought with Hebrew faith.

At one time Coleridge seems to have been tempted to found his whole metaphysic, as Schelling did, upon a theory of creative imagination, which, in overcoming the opposition of subject and object, "enables art to compass the impossible, to resolve an infinite contradiction in a finite product".[2] But he resisted this temptation, and his reason for doing so is significant. Schelling and his followers, he says, are guilty of a "confusion of the creaturely spirit in the great moments

---

[1] MS. cited by Alice D. Snyder, *Coleridge on Logic and Learning*, p. 129 n
[2] Schelling, *Werke*, Vol. III. p. 349.

of its renascence with the deific energies in Deity itself".[1] The Jew and the Greek were both strong in Coleridge, and he could not keep the peace between them. This I believe to be the secret of the prodigious scope and energy of his thought, and of his lameness in formal exposition. He worshipped the Hebrew God, a God of righteousness and the world's creator, long before he reached anything that could be called Christian orthodoxy; and all his life he felt impelled in his own fashion to justify God's ways to men. But to talk of God and man is to consider personal relations; a thing Coleridge was ill equipped to do. For when he made alliance with his German contemporaries, he committed himself to a monistic philosophy dedicated to the overpassing of relation: a philosophy grounded in the unitary consciousness, and progressing in terms of the continual reconstitution and enlargement of consciousness. In deserting Spinoza, Coleridge rejected a philosophy of purely immanent deity; but he found nothing in German Idealism whereby to redress the balance through a philosophy of divine transcendence. He was not blind to his position: indeed his largest achievement was to anticipate, in part, both Hegel and Kierkegaard's criticism of Hegel. And so he found no rest, but wandered ceaselessly; in love with identity and haunted by relation; always, as Dorothy Wordsworth described him, "in search of something new", but returning again and again to the meeting-place of Jew and Greek in the Alexandrian schools.

With Wordsworth the case is different. Recently, and especially in America, there has been a reaction against Arnold's summary dismissal of his philosophy. Scarcely anyone has been so rash as to claim system for

[1] J. H. Muirhead, *Coleridge as Philosopher*, p. 56, citing C.'s MS. note on Jacob Boehme's *Aurora*.

the whole body of his writing, but it has become almost modish to argue that in a particular poem or period of his life Wordsworth was under the influence of this or that philosopher; and then to study the work of master and disciple in close relation. Wordsworth himself gives no encouragement to this tendency: his references to philosophy are few and usually disparaging. He read little, and showed no interest in contemporary thought. Towards Kant and his successors his attitude was one of ignorant defiance: when taxed, late in life, with the question of Coleridge's plagiarisms, he declared that he had "never read a word of German metaphysics, thank Heaven!"[1]

But the matter is not so easily disposed of; for it is always possible that what he failed to read in books he heard from Coleridge: and when a critic claims to discover echoes of Plato, of the hermetical books, of Spinoza, of Shaftesbury, of Hartley, of Stoic and Kantian morality, of all sorts of mystical writings, he can appeal with perfect confidence to Coleridge's conversation. No doubt Coleridge said it all. And there can be no general denial of such a claim, because Wordsworth's work abounds in verbal echoes. What must be denied is that the existence of these echoes is enough to establish the tracing of intellectual debts as a valid critical method.

Concerning Wordsworth's philosophical borrowings, the first of his prose works is the one most in point. In 1793 he made an essay in political theory, in the form of an open letter to the Bishop of Llandaff, "on the extraordinary avowal of his Political Principles, contained in the Appendix to his late Sermon: by a Republican". Men were being persecuted at this time for the expression of radical opinions, and Wordsworth prudently did not publish his letter. The Bishop's

---

[1] *Correspondence of Crabb Robinson with the Wordsworth Circle* (ed. Edith J. Morley), Vol. I. p. 401.

Appendix is a feeble performance. It is inordinately complacent:

> The greatest freedom that can be enjoyed by man in a state of civil society, the greatest security that can be given him with respect to the protection of his character, property, personal liberty, limb, and life, is afforded to every individual by our present constitution.[1]

And it presents, in as crude a form as one could find, the conservative argument for orders established and unchangeable:

> I do not mean to speak of peasants and mechanics with any degree of disrespect; I am not so ignorant of the importance, either of the natural or social chain by which all the individuals of the human race are connected together, as to think disrespectfully of any link of it. Peasants and mechanics are as useful to the State as any other order of men; but their utility consists in their discharging well the duties of their respective stations; it ceases when they affect to become legislators; when they intrude themselves into concerns for which their education has not fitted them.[2]

Wordsworth does better than this. Not long before his letter was written, as he relates in *The Prelude*, he had been in London, listening to the great parliamentary orators of the day. And not without profit, for his letter is a good debating performance. The bishop had declared: "The courts of British justice are impartial and incorrupt; they respect not the persons of men; the poor man's lamb is, in their estimation, as sacred as the monarch's crown. . . ."[3] Wordsworth replies: "I congratulate your Lordship upon your enthusiastic fondness for the judicial proceedings of this country. I am happy to find you have passed

---

[1] A. B. Grosart, *Prose Works of W. Wordsworth*, Vol. I. p. 26.
[2] Grosart, Vol. I. p. 28.
[3] *Ibid.*, p. 26.

through life without having your fleece torn from your back in the thorny labyrinth of litigation."[1] There is personal bitterness here, for at this date Wordsworth's family was still trying, without any success, to recover a large sum of money of which Lord Lonsdale had wrongfully deprived them ten years earlier.

Wordsworth follows the radical pamphleteers of the time in his argument for universal suffrage and in his attack on the powers of the Crown and all kinds of hereditary privilege. But what he has to say he says clearly, and with an impassioned dignity of style characteristic of his best prose. Moreover, there is something very personal to Wordsworth in his appreciating thus soon the economic evils of the Industrial Revolution: it is a standpoint which he never abandoned, and which explains the radicalism that stayed with him until he died. Our legislators, says Wordsworth, who profess to hold private property inviolable,

> have unjustly left unprotected that most important part of property, not less real because it has no material existence, that which ought to enable the labourer to provide food for himself and his family. I appeal to innumerable statutes, whose constant and professed object it is to lower the price of labour, to compel the workman to be *content* with arbitrary wages, evidently too small from the necessity of legal enforcement of the acceptance of them. Even from the astonishing amount of the sums raised for the support of one description of the poor may be concluded the extent and greatness of that oppression, whose effects have rendered it possible for the few to afford so much, and have shown us that such a multitude of our brothers exist in even helpless indigence.[2]

There is good sense and fine writing in Wordsworth's letter; but he is no more a political philosopher than his opponent. He meets the bishop's naïve affirma-

[1] Grosart, Vol. I. p. 20.   [2] *Ibid.*, p. 16.

tion of the *status quo* with an equally ingenuous plea for revolution. More than once in his letter Wordsworth refers to Rousseau's master concept, the General Will. Rousseau himself works the General Will very hard: it is the means by which he seeks to reconcile a democratic theory of government with the doctrine of natural rights. He argues, in the tradition of Locke, that every individual in the state is the bearer of certain fundamental rights of which he cannot be deprived by any other man or by the state itself; but, unlike Locke, he is a democrat and must explain why the natural rights of the minority are not at the mercy of the ruling majority. It has sometimes been said, and often implied, that the General Will is an elaborate device for proving that the majority can do no wrong. But this is misleading: the General Will has been an idea of enormous influence because it faces two ways—backwards, towards the eighteenth-century school of natural law; and forwards, towards corporate theories of the state in which the words "majority" and "minority" suffer a sea change.

Wordsworth shows no sign of having understood Rousseau: what is much more important, he makes it quite clear that he does not think like a philosopher. His argument is robustly practical; and, although decked out in the terms of political theory, it never moves among intellectual abstractions. He defines republican laws as "the expression of the general will"[1]; but then, instead of considering the General Will and the mode of its self-expression in terms of law, he reasons, like a sensible policeman, that "a Republic has a manifest advantage over a Monarchy, in as much as less force is requisite to compel obedience to its laws".[2] Wordsworth's political writing has moral passion and an intense though often incoherent humanity; but it has no theoretical merits.

[1] Grosart, Vol. I. p. 12.   [2] *Ibid.*, p. 12.

The General Will does not matter because Wordsworth's use of it scarcely extends beyond verbal echo.
He knew the phrase, but did not see its point: nor,
probably, did he try, for his interest in politics was not
speculative. But there is another kind of indebtedness
which Wordsworth admitted and which he believed to
be important. He wrote to a friend, in March 1798,
when he was beginning to think about *The Recluse*: "If
you could collect for me any books of travels, you
would render me an essential service, as without much
of such reading my present labours cannot be brought
to a conclusion."[1] Here we have the encouragement
that is strikingly absent in the case of philosophy; and
Wordsworth's poetry bears him out to this extent, that
it shows wide and careful reading in the literature of
travel.

There is, for example, a passage in *The Prelude*
which, in its general tone of oriental delight and its
reference to "Domes of Pleasure", invites comparison
with *Kubla Khan*. We find in John Barrow's *Travels in
China*: "The Emperor was pleased to give directions
to his first minister to shew us his park or garden at
Gehol. It is called in Chinese Van-shoo-yuen, or the
Paradise of ten thousand trees. . . ."[2] And Wordsworth
speaks of the country where he was born as a

> tract more exquisitely fair
> Than is that Paradise of ten thousand Trees,
> Or Gehol's famous Gardens, in a Clime
> Chosen from widest empire, for delight
> Of the Tartarian Dynasty composed;
> (Beyond that mighty Wall, not fabulous,
> China's stupendous mound!) by patient skill
> Of myriads, and boon Nature's lavish help;
> Scene link'd to scene, an evergrowing change,

[1] *Early Letters of W. and Dorothy Wordsworth* (ed. de Selincourt), p. 188
[2] *Wordsworth's "Prelude"* (ed. de Selincourt), p. 550.

> Soft, grand, or gay! with Palaces and Domes
> Of Pleasure spangled over, shady Dells
> For Eastern Monasteries, sunny Mounds
> With Temples crested, Bridges, Gondolas,
> Rocks, Dens, and Groves. . . .[1]

What can be said of this? No more, I think, than that Wordsworth read travel books for the good reason that they interested him, and when he came himself to describe strange or fabulous lands he drew upon his reading. A Wordsworthian equivalent to *The Road to Xanadu* would be dull indeed; for Wordsworth lacked the entireness of mind that makes Coleridge's borrowing revelant to his poetry. Travel books were sources of information, and he reproduced what he wanted, in loose verse paraphrase. The result is not always a failure: Wordsworth's description of tropical scenery in *Ruth*, for which he is indebted to Bartram's *Travels*, could hardly be improved upon in simple vividness. But Wordsworthian scholarship remains in this respect a negative discipline: it teaches the unimportance of his, sources.

The story of Wordsworth's poetic debts has a similar beginning. At the age of fourteen he was set to write a poem in celebration of his school's second centenary. The result he later judged to be "but a tame imitation of Pope's versification".[2] And so it is: but to say no more is to deal harshly with a small boy's Heroics; for they have a certain alertness, and they catch the antithetical manner well enough to show that he had a quick ear for style:

> Oft have I said, the paths of Fame pursue,
> And all that Virtue dictates, dare to do;
> Go to the world, peruse the book of man,
> And learn from thence thy own defects to scan;

[1] Bk. VIII. 121.
[2] *Poetical Works* (ed. de Selincourt), Vol. I. p. 366.

Severely honest, break no plighted trust,
But coldly rest not here—be more than just. . . .[1]

In 1787, when he was sixteen, Wordsworth first published a poem, a sonnet *On seeing Miss Helen Maria
Williams weep at a tale of distress*. This also might be
called a tame imitation; but it differs from the centenary
poem in one important respect: Wordsworth has
abandoned the sense of Pope for the sensibility of Miss
Williams, a specialist in the poetry of feeling which
enjoyed a great vogue at this time and infested the
magazines with just such rubbish as Wordsworth's
sonnet:

She wept.—Life's purple tide began to flow
In languid streams through every thrilling vein;
Dim were my swimming eyes—my pulse beat slow,
And my full heart was swelled to dear delicious pain.

It is not at all extraordinary that a schoolboy should
imitate his elders. Wordsworth's early verse is none the
less remarkable in the extent to which it is pure copy—
much of it is direct translation or adaptation of Greek
and Latin originals—and in the diversity of its models.
Most of these were soon discarded; but Wordsworth
never outgrew the instinct to copy closely, as is
evidenced by his continuing interest in translation and
by the pains which he bestowed upon his modernized
versions of Chaucer.

This instinct, in itself a brute fact of which nothing
can be made, derives significance from its manifesting
the most vital quality of Wordsworth's mind—I mean
its literalness. Literalness is the necessary preface to his
genius. Everything, for him, was what it was, and it was
not anything else: the thing done or suffered, the thing
seen or heard or read, touched him because it was so.
In its being so he saw it as somehow self-guaranteeing

[1] *And Has the Sun . . .?*

—this was the heart of his naturalistic optimism; and yet to see things as they are he considered no easy matter, but the reward of vigilant devotion to the actual—and this was the burden of his greatest poetry. There is no escaping Wordsworth's literalness: it appears in the worst as well as in the best things he did. It betrays itself in his ill-considered appeal, when attacking poetic diction, to the "language really used by men", as more poetic than poetry; and much of his weakest verse stands as a monument to the delusion that he had done what was required of him if he stuck closely to the facts. Literalness is responsible for his profundity and narrowness alike. His obstinacy, his very limited powers of self-criticism, his feeble sense of humour, his plain dullness, are all attributable to it.

Because this literalness is everywhere, its kinds must be distinguished, and the difference made clear between what matters and what does not. The task is sometimes easy. Thus it would be patently absurd to explain the fair success of the poem *Stepping Westward* by the fact that it begins with the actual words of a greeting extended to Wordsworth when he was travelling in Scotland with Dorothy; or, on the other hand, to argue that *Simon Lee* is a failure because "the expression when the hounds were out, 'I dearly love their voices' was word for word from his own lips",[1] as Wordsworth tells us in his note to the poem. In both cases Wordsworth attached importance to the very words he heard, and he therefore held fast to them. In *Stepping Westward* he explains, effectively, why they mattered to him:

> The salutation had to me
> The very sound of courtesy:
> Its power was felt. . . .

[1] *P.W.*, Vol. IV. p. 413.

But in *Simon Lee* he is too intent upon an accurate recording of the facts to explain anything, and the result is a disaster:

> And he is lean and he is sick;
> His body, dwindled and awry,
> Rests upon ankles swoln and thick;
> His legs are thin and dry.
> One prop he has, and only one,
> His wife, an aged woman,
> Lives with him, near the waterfall,
> Upon the village Common.

But the utterances that caught Wordsworth's attention are both external to his poems: they are occasions for poetry, and everything depends on what is made of them.

This is simple enough. But when the sovereign quality of Wordsworth's mind reveals itself in purely literary debts, the distinction between relevant and irrelevant becomes much more subtle. There is a very early work, written probably when Wordsworth was sixteen, which I shall quote in full. By no means a good poem, it has things of interest in it; and the problem is made neat by the fact that we are concerned with indebtedness to a single poet, Milton, and a single poem, *Lycidas*. Wordsworth's elegy on a drowned dog opens thus:

> Where were ye, nymphs, when the remorseless deep
> Clos'd o'er your little favourite's hapless head?
> For neither did ye mark with solemn dread[1]
> In Derwent's rocky woods the white Moonbeam
> Pace like a Druid o'er the haunted steep;
> Nor in Winander's stream.[2]

[1] Professor de Selincourt's text has "dream", but the sense and the rhyme scheme seem to require "dread". In Wordsworth's MS. the page is torn and the last letter of this word is missing.

[2] *P.W.*, Vol. I. p. 264.

This looks like parody. Wordsworth, one might at once suppose, is warning us in the first two lines that he is being deliberately absurd at the expense of *Lycidas*; the absurdity heightened by the way Milton degenerates into the diction of eighteenth-century Miltonic as soon as the very words of *Lycidas* are abandoned, at "little favourite's hapless head". The skilfully managed short line and the echo of Milton's "steep Where your old bards, the famous Druids, lie", point to the same conclusion. But Wordsworth is not being funny: it was not in his nature to regard his own literalness as amusing or ridiculous. And there is more here than Milton. Let us isolate the simile:

> For neither did ye mark . . . the white Moonbeam
> Pace like a Druid. . . .

Milton's similes have an extended splendour: in their slow unfolding they enforce the relentless, even thrust of his verse. But this simile does not march. "White", which appears at first the conventional monosyllabic adjective needed for "moonbeam", gains suddenly in strength from its literal applicability to "Druid". And "pace", while plainly descriptive of "Druid", is startling in relation to its own subject. Wordsworth has so strengthened the second term of his comparison that it cannot be taken as in any way dependent on the first: the whole is instantly reread with the terms inverted, and because of this double movement, animate and inanimate are held in urgent and reciprocal relationship, the tension of which is accentuated by the line end pause and by the unexpected stress on "pace" which makes a fulcrum of the verb. There is an odd compactness by virtue of which Wordsworth's simile looks like a metaphor; and it has the same quality, although it is not so closely wrought, as

> The cataracts blow their trumpets from the steep

in the Immortality Ode. And yet this metaphor, in the deliberateness with which its relations are managed, itself looks curiously like a simile. This is the Wordsworthian middle air which must later be explored.

There follow, in Wordsworth's poem, four lines of eighteenth-century miltonizing, in the manner of *L'Allegro:*

> Then did ye swim with sportive smile
> From fairy-templed isle to isle,
> Which hear her far-off ditty sweet
> Yet feel not ev'n the milkmaid's feet.

And then:

> What tho' he still was at my side
> When, lurking near, I there have seen
> Your faces white, your tresses green,
> Like water lilies floating on the tide?

Wordsworth suddenly wrenches the poem from its remote mythological context by means of the visual appropriateness of the water lilies: he says "I there have seen"; and through the exactness of the simile he makes good his claim. Milton does not risk the ruin of *Lycidas* by pretending to see his nymphs, or anything else. His flowers are enamelled pageant-flowers, and their names are recited by a herald.

The poem continues:

> He saw not, bark'd not, he was still
> As the soft moonbeam sleeping on the hill,
> Or when ah! cruel maids, ye stretched him stiff and chill.

Again the simile is interesting; in the first place because of its connexion with Milton's line:

> And now the Sun had stretched out all the hills.

This is the only convincing visual image in *Lycidas*, and on that account likely to hold Wordsworth's attention. Furthermore, Milton manages the vowels of his line with extreme virtuosity—a skill which Wordsworth was quick to admire and to emulate, as in the famous *Prelude* lines on Spenser:

> Sweet Spenser, moving through his clouded heaven
> With the moon's beauty and the moon's soft pace. . . .[1]

Finally, the word "stretch'd" had a literal importance for Wordsworth. He wanted it, in perfect seriousness, for his dog, and he introduced it himself in the next line. As in the case of the druid and the moonbeam, Wordsworth is relating animate and inanimate; but here the relation is different. This simile is less highly organized than the other, and not so tense. "Soft" has no reference beyond "moonbeam", and in any case it is a careless choice, in its suggestion of relaxation and warmth, with "stiff and chill" following immediately. "Still" does nothing to the simile, because it is wide enough to cover both terms in a general and lazy way, without any stress. "Sleeping" appears at a glance to be playing a part in this simile like that of "pace" in the first. But this is not so. "Pace", lying between the two terms, is figurative and violent, and, helped by "white", compels them towards interaction. "Sleeping", on the other hand, succeeds both terms, which are referred simultaneously to it, as a fixed point equidistant from the dead dog and the motionless patch of light. The structure of the simile and the theme of stillness in death work together for a geometrical, not a dynamic relation.

Wordsworth ends his poem:

> If, while I gaz'd to Nature blind,
> In the calm Ocean of my mind
> Some new-created image rose

[1] Bk. III. 281.

In full-grown beauty at its birth
Lovely as Venus from the sea,
Then, while my glad hand sprung to thee,
We were the happiest pair on earth.

We noticed, regarding the nymphs and the water
lilies, the opposition of an impossible, mythological
world and an observed world of nature. Here the mind
is a seascape, over against the mobile, earth-born
relationship of boy and dog; and the sudden, perfect
form of the mental image is emphasized by the classical
allusion. This is a little grotesque, and it seems un-
likely that Wordsworth had any clear idea of what he
was doing. But he remembered the passage, and when
he came in *The Prelude* to describe how he composed
poetry while walking with his dog, he turned to it
again:

this Dog was used
To watch me, an attendant and a friend
Obsequious to my steps, early and late,
Though often of such dilatory walk
Tired, and uneasy at the halts I made.
A hundred times when, in these wanderings,
I have been busy with the toil of verse,
Great pains and little progress, and at once
Some fair enchanting image in my mind
Rose up, full-form'd, like Venus from the sea
Have I sprung forth towards him, and let loose
My hand upon his back with stormy joy,
Caressing him again, and yet again.
And when, in the public roads at eventide
I saunter'd, like a river murmuring
And talking to itself, at such a season
It was his custom to jog on before;
But, duly, whensoever he had met
A passenger approaching, would he turn
To give me timely notice, and straitway,

> Punctual to such admonishment, I hush'd
> My voice, composed my gait, and shap'd myself
> To give and take a greeting that might save
> My name from piteous rumours, such as wait
> On men suspected to be craz'd in brain.[1]

The contrast between inner and outer, hurried and uncertain in the early poem, is now developed with entire
success. Each world authenticates the other; and the
dog, as he trots before the poet—a premonition, this,
of Wordsworth's full power—mediates between them.

Within its very modest limits, this immature, patch-
work poem foreshadows the kind of complexity in
which Wordsworth's literalmindedness involves us.
Direct verbal correspondences, even with poetry near
to his heart, may mean very little. There is another
phrase of Milton's, again from *Lycidas*, which is echoed
three times in Wordsworth's work. Milton wrote:

> But, O the heavy change, now thou art gone,
> Now thou art gone, and never must return!

And in the 1805 text of *The Prelude* we find:

> To me [be] the grief confined that Thou art gone
> From this last spot of earth where Freedom now
> Stands single in her only sanctuary,
> A lonely wanderer, art gone, by pain
> Compell'd and sickness, at this latter day,
> This heavy time of change for all mankind. . . .[2]

This is almost certainly an accident, occasioned by the
rhythm of the first line, with the phrase "thou art
gone" at the end of it, and by the repetition of "art
gone" three lines later. It may have been the realization of having unconsciously followed Milton that led
Wordsworth to replace "this heavy time of change"

---

[1] *The Prelude*, Bk. IV. 96.   [2] Bk. X. 981.

by "this sorrowful reverse" when he revised *The Prelude*.

"Heavy change" also appears in the third book of *The Excursion*:

> with a holier love inspired, I looked
> On her—at once superior to my woes
> And partner of my loss—O heavy change!
> Dimness o'er this clear luminary crept
> Insensibly. . . .[1]

And again this is probably unintended: for language and context are very Miltonic, in fact directly suggestive of *Paradise Lost*.

The third occurrence is both unimportant and unhappy. Milton is interpolated in the midst of a tumbling Lyrical Ballad:

> But, oh the heavy change!—bereft
> Of health, strength, friends, and kindred, see!
> Old Simon to the world is left
> In liveried poverty![2]

This invoking of *Lycidas* in a purely external fashion defeats the declared purpose of Wordsworth's ballad, which is to be in the conventional sense unpoetic: it introduces exactly the wrong literary associations. Wordsworth is often attracted towards the words themselves in a way that prevents him from asking whether the present context is suitable: he is a magpie-poet, seizing any bright object that catches his eye, dropping it into his nest. In his maturity he borrows less frequently in this direct fashion, and with more discrimination; but he still resorts all too often to a set of well-worn devices, mainly rhetorical and Miltonic, with which to coax himself along.

[1] Bk. III. 667.   [2] *Simon Lee.*

c

Wordsworth's poem on the drowned dog shows him indulging his taste for quotation. It also shows him thinking as well as writing in the Miltonic mode—a submission to Milton's influence that runs very deep, and becomes as much a matter of entire attitude as of expression. Hence, often, the authority of his Miltonic blank verse:

> Sometimes, more sternly mov'd, I would relate
> How vanquish'd Mithridates northward pass'd,
> And, hidden in the cloud of years, became
> That Odin, Father of a Race, by whom
> Perish'd the Roman Empire....[1]

This was how he felt about heroic themes; not less genuinely because Milton was in part responsible.

Wordsworth's poem also introduces the problem of originality. His way of comparing a moonbeam and a druid, then a moonbeam and a dead dog, I take for the sign of a most singular vision of the world, of its substantial ghostliness and its alliances in diversity. The mind's seascape and the Venus-Thoughts seem to me even more prophetic; for his understanding of the relationship of inner and outer is Wordsworth's principal claim to greatness. He had something new to say about mental and physical.

Even so, Wordsworth's originality is not easily approached. He enclosed his finest performance in a husk so tough and commonplace as to mislead bad critics and distress good ones. And although there is some sort of anthology agreement as to what is best, the rest is almost silence. Even Coleridge and Arnold could do little more than point, in their different ways, towards his best work, implying that it rises unaccountable from level wastes of mediocrity. Arnold thought Wordsworth was a kind of Scholar Gipsy, which I

---

[1] *The Prelude,* Bk. I. 185.

reckoned a mistake: while Coleridge regarded him as a
philosophical poet who failed to realize his full powers.

Wondering what Coleridge meant, we are faced
with his very liberal use of the word philosophy: he
believed that all good poets must also be good philosophers. Nor is it clear what Coleridge understood by
the philosophical character of poetry. He relates poetry
in a very general way to his own variety of voluntaristic
Idealism, as demonstrating both the primacy of will
and the possibility of intuitive knowledge. Here and
there, in his references to the "union and interpenetra-
tion of universal and particular"[1] in Shakespeare's
characters, and to Shakespeare's dramatic presentation
of "the *homo generalis* not as an abstraction from
observation of a variety of men, but as a substance
capable of endless modifications",[2] Coleridge hints at
his reason for thinking Shakespeare the greatest of
philosophers: he has in mind something like a poetic
manifestation of the Hegelian Concrete Universal. But
this is all much too vague. Fortunately he is more
precise about Wordsworth. There is a remark which he
repeats several times, with slight variation: Wordsworth is a philosophical poet because of "the contem-
plative position, which is peculiarly—perhaps I might
say exclusively—fitted for him. His proper title is
Spectator ab extra".[3] Although Wordsworth is capable
of the most profound sympathy "with man as man",
his is the sympathy of "a contemplator rather than a
fellow-sufferer": he feels "for, never with" his subject.[4] There is, then, a detachment natural to Wordsworth which does not prevent him feeling strongly

---

[1] *The Friend* (4th ed.), Vol. III. p. 116.
[2] *Coleridge's Miscellaneous Criticism* (ed. T. M. Raysor), pp. 43-4.
[3] *Table Talk*, July 31, 1832.
[4] *Biographia Literaria* (ed. J. Shawcross), Vol. II. p. 122.

about his subject. This is the best of introductions to Wordsworth; and, since it is said by way of implied contrast with himself, to Coleridge also.

Coleridge's philosophy of the Great and the Whole is relevant to the entire man. His love of identity, of a speculative system through which the distinctness of his own individuality might be transcended, is no intellectual game, but the expression of a longing, born of great pain, to ease the burden of differentiated existence, to lose himself in higher synthesis, to be possessed by God. As in his approach to deity, so in his dealings with the world, Coleridge clung to his Idealism with more than intellectual loyalty. Wordsworth remarked of him that "he was not under the influence of natural objects"[1]; and Coleridge said the same thing of himself, in the form of an apparent paradox: "The further I ascend from animated Nature . . . the greater becomes in me the intensity of the feeling of life." The quality both of his imagination and his intelligence was determined by the force with which reality was borne in upon him as mind. He suffered terribly on that account in his dreams—"the very Substances", he called them, "and foot-thick calamities of my life"; and he defined Nightmare, with a pathetic pedantry, as "*terror corporeus sive materialis*".[2] His few great poems reflect the horror and the vivid completeness of the life which he lived within the mind: they reflect also his dread of isolation as a state of helplessness and vulnerability. Certainly Coleridge's proper title was not *Spectator ab extra*.

This dread of isolation is therefore both imaginative and intellectual. To be wholly conscious of one's distinctness, he said, is "to be betrayed into the wretchedness of *division*".[3] Division was intellectually wretched to him because it was unintelligible: he felt

[1] Grosart, Vol. III. p. 442.
[2] *Anima Poetae* (ed. E. H. Coleridge), p. 245.   [3] *Ibid.*, p. 184.

unable to talk about it without falling into a relational mode of thought which he recognized as the characteristic vice of eighteenth-century empiricism, and which he left behind him for ever when he set sail for a new philosophical world of rational synthesis.

Coleridge was not born a nineteenth-century Idealist: it was only after long hesitation that he finally turned his back on the British empirical tradition. A few months before Wordsworth and he became close friends, Coleridge named his eldest son after David Hartley, his acknowledged master in philosophy since his undergraduate days at Cambridge. Hartley was himself a disciple of Locke, an expounder of a fanciful physiology of mind and of a most intemperate version of the theory of association of ideas—a thinker small in talent who gained a short-lived celebrity by saying with vulgar emphasis the things that his generation wanted to hear. He combined, incongruously, a humdrum Christian orthodoxy with a show of scientific method directed to a deterministic, or a necessitarian interpretation of human nature. The young Coleridge was in search of a Christian philosophy, and he fell, as he continued all his life to fall, an easy victim to scientific quackery. It is because he wore the manners of his age with comic exaggeration that Hartley is an important figure in Coleridge's philosophical history: the abandonment of Hartley meant the abandonment of a way of thinking deeply entrenched in England since Bacon's *Advancement of Learning;* or, as Coleridge himself expressed it, viewing his crisis in even larger perspective, the return from Aristotle and the conceptionists to Plato and Idealism.

Hartley Coleridge was born in 1796; and Coleridge's disenchantment with David Hartley extended throughout 1797 and 1798, the years of his first and closest intimacy with Wordsworth. For Coleridge they were years of extreme unrest. He turned to Berkeley, after whom he named his second son; to Spinoza, to St Paul and the Fourth Gospel. Germany lay before him. Kant had not yet caught hold of him "with giant hands", nor Fichte and Schelling suggested the way beyond Kant. The shape of the new world was not clear to him, but the old was fast becoming uninhabitable. At this time he came to know Wordsworth and to think him capable of writing the "only true philosophical poem in existence". Wordsworth's poetry made an immediate and strong impression upon him because it referred directly to his own predicament: it revealed Wordsworth moving with obvious assurance through country in which he himself was losing all sense of direction; and thus it was that Wordsworth gained his greatest disciple. This is not to say that Coleridge supposed Wordsworth to be doing the same thing that Locke and Hartley had done, and to be doing it better. He knew very well that "when philosophy paints its grey monochrome some form of life has grown old, and it cannot by this grey in grey be made young again, but only known".[1] In the utterance of a great poet Coleridge witnessed not a world's illumination merely, but the palingenesis of its youth; for the work of Wordsworth's early maturity is the last and finest achievement of the eighteenth-century imagination. This important truth has not been appreciated, principally because Coleridge was at no time securely possessed of it himself; and the further he travelled into the nineteenth century the less able and willing he became to remember what had originally impelled him towards Wordsworth. As he grew unmindful of the other's sources of power he came, I shall argue, to demand impossibilities of him. But some things Coleridge always saw clearly, and the most vital of these was Wordsworth's isolation, his proper title of *Spectator ab extra*.

[1] Hegel, Preface to *Philosophie des Rechts*.

Coleridge himself discussed Wordsworth's isolation in terms of sexual psychology: "of all the men I ever knew, Wordsworth has the least femineity in his mind. He is *all* man. He is a man of whom it might have been said, 'It is good for him to be alone'."[1] The instinct to stand guard over its boundaries, to assert its distinctness, Coleridge considered the first indication of a masculine mind, and one supremely obvious in Wordsworth's. Certainly there was a self-centredness about him peculiarly masculine. This appears immediately as an aspect of weakness; of a narrow egotism betraying itself in his readiness to pontificate, in complacent moralizing, in a certain roughness in his dealings with others: all these accentuated by the retired life that he led, presiding over a household of attentive women.

Both Keats and Hazlitt made this egotism the ground of hostile criticism, but realized dimly, as did Coleridge, that it was merely a part of the much larger issue of Wordsworth's isolation. Keats suggested two basic types of poetic genius in his categories of the Wordsworthian or Egotistical Sublime and of Negative Capability. Hazlitt, in his review of *The Excursion*, wrote that "an intense intellectual egotism swallows up everything"; he noted the level tone, the quality of monologue in Wordsworth's verse, and he marvelled at the way Wordsworth turns inward for nourishment. "The power of his mind preys upon itself. It is as if there were nothing but himself and the universe. He lives in the busy solitude of his own heart; in the deep silence of thought." Hazlitt's account of his first meeting with Wordsworth still bears quotation:

> I think I see him now. He answered in some degree to his friend's description of him, but was more gaunt and Don Quixote-like. He was quaintly dressed (according to the

[1] *Table Talk and Omniana* (ed. T. Ashe), p. 339.

costume of that unconstrained period) in a brown fustian jacket and striped pantaloons. There was something of a roll, a lounge in his gait, not unlike his own Peter Bell. There was a severe, worn pressure of thought about his temples, a fire in his eye (as if he saw something in objects more than the outward appearance), an intense high narrow forehead. . . .[1]

The reference to Don Quixote, suggesting as it does the sublime absurdity of a self-appointed task pursued with utter singleness of purpose, beyond delusion to a kind of lonely sanity, is more appropriate than perhaps Hazlitt intended. But Hazlitt certainly did gain the impression of strenuous and solitary thought. So did Carlyle, when he met Wordsworth forty years later:

His face bore marks of much, not always peaceful meditation, the look of it not bland or benevolent so much as close impregnable and hard. . . .[2]

And occasionally, in the correspondence of his later years, we catch a glimpse of the "desolate-minded" old man of local tradition, the silent walker with "no pleasure in his face",[3] much oppressed by the difficulty of communicating even with those he loved, and anxious to discover how he must appear to others:

And now my dear Friend I should like to let loose my heart upon this scrap of paper—but it is folly to think of it. Mary has already told you how deeply we love you and how ardently we long for your return, though for my own part I must say that increasing years are I feel making me less and less of an interesting companion. Nothing however said or done to me for some time has in relation to myself given me so much pleasure as a casual word of Anna's that the expres-

[1] *My First Acquaintance with Poets.*
[2] *Reminiscences.*
[3] H. D. Rawnsley, *Reminiscences of Wordsworth among the Peasantry of Westmorland,* published in *Wordsworthiana* (ed. William Knight).

sion of my face was ever varying. I had begun to fear that it
had lately been much otherwise.[1]

Solitude is the theme of Wordsworth's long life. It
is also the preoccupation of his poetry. Long before he
reached old age, he came to accept his solitude as a
condition imposed upon him in the natural course of
things, an appointed burden to be borne uncomplain-
ingly. But it had not always been thus. In his youth he
sought solitude with his whole heart, and he makes it
quite clear, in *The Prelude* and elsewhere, that he
sought it as the means of poetic grace. The power to
write poetry, he says many times, depended for him
upon the power to be alone. This points to a truth that
is everywhere recognized: Wordsworth's best poetry
deals with lonely places and solitary people, whereas
he was easily daunted into silence by crowds. It also
suggests a more difficult conclusion of which Coleridge,
Hazlitt and Keats were all aware.

Wordsworth was not primarily concerned with solitude as physical isolation. Solitude in this limited sense
is not unimportant, but its significance lies in his use of
it as the token of a peculiarly Wordsworthian seriousness, an outward sign of a state of mind casting its
shadow over a whole poem.

> On Man on Nature, and on Human Life,
> Musing in solitude. . . .

In this, the opening phrase of the Preface to *The
Excursion*, which Wordsworth wished to be regarded
as a "kind of Prospectus" to the entire *Recluse*, the
word solitude plays the part of key signature in music:
and I am sure that Wordsworth is here acting with the
deliberation of a composer in his choice of key. Indeed,
in two famous studies of solitude—*The Leech-Gatherer*
and *I wandered lonely as a cloud*—he conceals the truth,

---

[1] *Letters* (ed. de Selincourt), 1841-50, p. 1132.

in defiance of his own principle of fidelity to fact, that
he was not alone.

Having introduced himself as "musing in solitude",
Wordsworth at once reveals his deeper purpose. He is
writing, he says,

> Of the individual Mind that keeps her own
> Inviolate retirement. . . .

The solitude of which he is speaking issues from an
attitude towards personality; from an eagerness to
accept the fact that I am myself just because I am not
anything else: to be me is to be always apart. The final
barrier which is differentiated existence, dreadful to
Coleridge, is embraced by Wordsworth as the source
of enlightenment and strength. "Inviolate retirement"
sounds a note of exultation because the poet believes
that the way to wisdom lies through the individual's
awareness of his individuality. When he considers his
fitness to undertake *The Recluse*, Wordsworth makes
this awareness his starting-point:

> Possessions have I that are solely mine,
> Something within which yet is shared by none,
> Not even the nearest to me and most dear,
> Something which power and effort may impart. . . .[1]

His discovery of himself in his solitude has universal
consequences: it leads him to the poetic and effective
understanding of all things:

> Points have we all of us within our souls,
> Where all stand single; this I feel, and make
> Breathings for incommunicable powers.[2]

In Wordsworth's poetry his own and his neighbour's private strength is developed into a philosophy
that can be expressed in terms both of solitude and of
relationship. The large and lazy assumption that the

[1] *P.W.*, Vol. V. p. 336.   [2] *The Prelude:* Bk. III. 186.

Romantic poets were all striving to express unity has obscured the structure of distinct but related things which is the world of Wordsworth. When he describes his education for poetry in the early books of *The Prelude*, he lays stress on the power to distinguish:

> I had an eye
> Which in my strongest workings, evermore
> Was looking for the shades of difference
> As they lie hid in all exterior forms. . . .[1]

The insight and joy of his childhood were derived

> From manifold distinctions, differences
> Perceived in things, where to the common eye,
> No difference is. . . .[2]

And elsewhere he states that the strength of the impression made by objects depends upon the distinctness with which they are individually imagined:

> While yet a child, and long before his time
> He had perceived the presence and the power
> Of greatness, and deep feelings had impressed
> Great objects on his mind, with portraiture
> And colour so distinct, that on his mind
> They lay like substances, and almost seemed
> To haunt the bodily sense.[3]

There is nothing of conventional romantic haze.

The *Spectator ab extra* does not move towards his object; he never clutches, he shows no eagerness to merge. "I gazed and gazed," "I looked and looked," "I stared and listened"—phrases of this kind, and they are many, at once suggests his authorship. In the poetry of the Great Decade Wordsworth is involved in a huge, sustained argument from solitude to relationship, from the points "where all stand single" to their connexions

---

[1] Bk. III. 156.   [2] Bk. II. 318.
[3] *P.W.*, Vol. V. p. 381. Compare *The Excursion:* Bk. I. 134.

with each other. And here there can be no substitute
for his poetry: the interdependence of true solitude and
true relationship was for Wordsworth a final issue
engaging his full powers and manageable only in poetic
terms. This interdependence makes an uncertain basis,
even for his own critical judgments:

> Having had the good fortune to be born and reared in a
> mountainous country, from my very childhood I have felt
> the falsehood that pervades the volumes imposed upon the
> world under the name of Ossian. From what I saw with my
> own eyes, I knew that the imagery was spurious. In nature
> everything is distinct, but nothing defined into absolute
> independent singleness. In Macpherson's work, it is exactly
> the reverse; everything (that is not stolen) is in this manner
> defined, insulated, dislocated, deadened—yet nothing
> distinct.[1]

Wordsworth must find another way of opposing the
thing single and the thing distinct.

What is a thing? How is one thing related to other
things? Wordsworth would not have framed his questions in quite the way he did, had he not grown up in
the eighteenth century; nor would his metaphysical
enquiry have been thus childlike in its unembarrass-
ment had he possessed the intellectual selfconsciousness
of a philosopher. This very innocence lends importance
to his inherited forms of thought: it allowed him to
give general assent to the assumptions of the age. He
accepted the problem as it had been stated by the
eighteenth century: in doubt or in extremity he did not,
like Coleridge, attempt restatement. Rather, he persisted in the old questions; and hence the monotony of
his genius.

There is thus a conservatism in the context of
Wordsworth's thought. He is not in revolt against the

[1] Essay Supplementary to the Preface to the 1815 Edition of Wordsworth's Poems.

Great Machine, the master-image of eighteenth-
century science and philosophy. Only the phrase is unwordsworthian (though there is enough of pure
eighteenth-century poetic in him to allow a reference
to his wife's spirit, in relation to her body, as "the very
pulse of the machine"[1]): he would prefer something
more supple, like "this universal frame of things". His
complaint is that nobody has as yet observed its com-
ponent parts with sufficiently devoted care, or
experienced fully the power and beauty of its movement.

In *The Prelude* Wordsworth uses the word "things"
with astonishing frequency. The Concordance reveals
that the 1850 text alone accounts for about one-third
of its occurrences in the entire bulk of his poetry. "I
looked for universal things"; "I conversed with things
that really are"; Wordsworth will make his verse "deal
boldly with substantial things"—the word is clearly
and consistently referred to the main theme of the
poem.[2] His search for universal things is on one side
a search for particularity: in his insistence upon con-
stancy, boundedness, irreducibility, he betrays the
imaginative impression of a traditional English
materialism. But he is more than a materialist, in that
he enquires not only for the particular but for the
powerful. Here his resources are heavily taxed. In
order to express essential energy, he is too often led to
personify spirit, motion, power itself, in a context of
vague declamation. But it is unfair to take this separation of effort at all seriously: Wordsworth is neither
atomist nor animist, in any sense that matters. His
problem comprehends both particularity and power;
and it is pursued through a Wordsworthian royal line
of solitary wanderers, from the Old Cumberland
Beggar to the White Doe of Rylstone.

[1] *She Was a Phantom of Delight.* . . .
[2] Bk.III. 110. Bk. II. 412. Bk. XII. 234.

Because Wordsworth saw the world as an intelligible complex—"frame" is his favourite term—and yet was neither pure materialist nor pure idealist, it may fairly be argued that his closest philosophical link was with Spinoza. And this is an illuminating comparison, provided imaginative kinship be not confounded with formal allegiance. Both were possessed of intense ethical passion; both talked much of virtue and wisdom as a discipline (critics have noted the Judaic quality of *Michael* and other narrative poems); both had the same instinctive reaction to the Cartesian problem of matter and mind, admitting difference but denying opposition. Above all, both were monists. Wordsworth was nearer to Spinoza than he was to Locke and Hartley because, while not fundamentally at odds with the Great Machine, he could not accept the Great Mechanic. It is a significant point of emphasis that Wordsworth was not attracted towards any particular religion of divine immanence, but was repelled by the crude transcendence of eighteenth-century deity. The Great Mechanic, or Paley's Divine Watchmaker, could render a satisfactory account of creation, as he sat back and admired his craftsmanship. But Wordsworth was not curious about creation. In fact, even when he had become in most things orthodox, he still disliked talking about God as Creator. I do not, he says, in a letter written in 1814,

> consider the Supreme Being as bearing the same relation to the Universe, as a watch-maker bears to a watch. In fact, there is nothing in the course of the religious education adopted in this country, and in the use made by us of the Holy Scriptures, that appears to me so injurious as perpetually talking about *making* by God . . . for heaven's sake, in your religious talk with children, say as little as possible about *making*.[1]

---

[1] *Letters* (ed. de Selincourt), 1811-20, p. 619.

Wordsworth did not want a philosophical *deus ex machina* whereby to explain how the world was made: he was face to face with suffering and love, the vast consequences of will and passion. And so we find in Wordsworth's early work an eighteenth-century cosmology unassociated with eighteenth-century theology: the alliance which professional philosophers of the school of Locke were able to sustain was a lie in the soul, intolerable to him. A vague awareness of tension encouraged him in the anti-intellectualism of his early years; and, although he had no precise notion of the intellectual issues involved, there is sometimes audible in his poetry a kind of prose voice, insisting on the gulf between Creator and created:

> In such access of mind, in such high hour
> Of visitation from the living God,
> He did not feel the God; he felt his works. . . .[1]

This gulf his poetry denies; not positively, by argument for pantheism, but negatively, by showing that the world can give a good account of itself. In the 1805 *Prelude*, the phrase "God and Nature's single sovereignty"[2] is not Spinozistic: it constitutes Wordsworth's refusal to shift his gaze from the "here" of "this green earth" to the "there" of an eighteenth-century heaven. His eye was firmly on the object which, as he then believed, would yield its secret entire:

> the very world which is the world
> Of all of us—the place where in the end,
> We find our happiness, or not at all![3]

It needs to be said that Wordsworth is very little concerned with God in the early *Prelude*: in fact he suggests as much himself; for he explains more than once that his concern in *The Recluse* will be with man

---

[1] *P.W.*, Vol. V. p. 382.   [2] Bk.IX. 237.
[3] 1850; Bk. XI. 142.

and nature, but he makes no reference to God. "My object," he wrote in 1798, "is to give pictures of Nature, Man, and Society. Indeed I know not anything which will not come within the scope of my plan."[1] Divinity, we find, is invoked most sparingly, like an organ stop to be used only for sublime and terrible effect:

> And here, O Friend! have I retraced my life
> Up to an eminence, and told a tale
> Of matters which, not falsely, I may call
> The glory of my youth. Of Genius, Power,
> Creation and Divinity itself
> I have been speaking, for my theme has been
> What pass'd within me.[2]

The plan thus outlined in 1798 was partially executed in the 1805 text of *The Prelude*. How long Wordsworth himself continued to regard *The Prelude* as part of *The Recluse* is not certain. Coleridge still spoke of it as *The Recluse* in 1804, and when the 1805 text was read to him he composed a poem in praise of it[3] which is written with discrimination, in spite of its rapturous tone, and reflects Wordsworth's original design for *The Recluse*. Coleridge points to the central humanism of *The Prelude*, and to its presentation of man and nature as eternally engaged in some wholly meaningful dialogue. The success of *The Prelude*, he says—and this is a very revealing admission—, reminds him of the ways in which he himself had failed. He calls upon Wordsworth as

> my comforter and guide!
> Strong in thyself, and powerful to give strength!

and in an eye-taking phrase, "the dread watch-tower of man's absolute self", he refers to Wordsworth's dis-

---

[1] *Early Letters* (ed. de Selincourt), p. 188.
[2] *The Prelude*, Bk. III. 168.
[3] *To William Wordsworth.*

covery of strength in solitude. Most striking, especially in Coleridge, is the omission to make Christian claims of any kind for *The Prelude;* or, indeed, to make Christian demands upon it. When he came, nine years later, to criticize *The Excursion,* things were very different; and Coleridge's dissatisfaction with *The Excursion* makes a convenient approach to the problem of Wordsworth's decline.

In May 1815 Coleridge wrote Wordsworth a careful letter in which he explained why *The Excursion* had disappointed him. He states in this letter[1] that his poem about *The Prelude* gives an accurate account of his feelings at that time, and that he had hoped that *The Prelude* and *The Excursion* would together form "one complete whole", although "in matter, form, and product to be different, each not only a distinct but a different work". It is, however, clear, that if Coleridge's expectations had been fulfilled, Wordsworth would have written a poem at once different from *The Prelude* and a contradiction of it. Coleridge hoped for a Christian poem treating of the Fall of Man and the Redemption. Wordsworth, he anticipated, was "to have affirmed a Fall in some sense, as a fact, the possibility of which cannot be understood from the nature of the will, but the reality of which is attested by experience and conscience". Such a poem would have denied not merely the optimism of *The Prelude,* from a Christian standpoint its Pelagianism, but the whole universe in which it moves. Paradise is here, or it is nowhere; and if it is here, there can have been no Fall: this imaginative monism at the heart of Wordsworth's poetry is more important than either optimism or pessimism. The world of Wordsworth's early tragedy, *The Borderers,* is related in Suffering; that of *The Prelude,* in Beauty and Fear; that of Wordsworth's Stoical middle years, in Duty: his statement of the relational

---

[1] *Letters* (ed. E. H. Coleridge), Vol. II. pp. 643-50.

D

principle changes, but his view of reality as a single intelligible structure persists. While this is so, there can be no effective dealing with the supernatural, and Coleridge's demands must remain impossible to meet. Sometimes, as we shall see, Wordsworth asked the impossible of himself, in attempting to write Christian poetry before he had acquired the power to do so: this is an aspect of decline. Eighteenth-century cosmology had firm hold of him, and he lacked the agility of mind that would have helped him to shift his position. For a long time he was both a Christian and a man in search of a sovereign and internal principle, beyond Euclid and Newton, beyond the theory of Necessity and the Association of Ideas, wherein to relate the elements of his own version of the Great Machine.

Coleridge explains that his disappointment with *The Excursion* is due partly to Wordsworth's failure to write the Christian poem he had hoped for, and partly to his refusal to strive towards certain philosophical conclusions. He had expected Wordsworth

> to have laid a solid and immoveable foundation for the edifice by removing the sandy sophisms of Locke, and the mechanic dogmatists, and demonstrating that the senses were living growths and developments of the mind and spirit, in a much juster as well as higher sense, than the mind can be said to be formed by the senses.

This is sufficiently precise to show that Coleridge was unaware of the extent to which his path had diverged from Wordsworth's since the time of their early friendship. He assumed that Wordsworth will speak out, like a post-Kantian Idealist, bent on

> the substitution of life and intelligence . . . for the philosophy of mechanism, which, in everything that is most worthy of the human intellect, strikes *Death*, and cheats itself by mistaking clear images for distinct conceptions, and which

idly demands conceptions where intuitions alone are possible
or adequate to the majesty of the Truth.

But Coleridge could have discovered, in the Preface to
The Excursion, Wordsworth's own account of what he
intended to say:

> my voice proclaims
> How exquisitely the individual Mind
> (And the progressive powers perhaps no less
> Of the whole species) to the external World
> Is fitted:—and how exquisitely, too—
> Theme this but little heard of among men—
> The external World is fitted to the Mind. . . .

Wordsworth is arguing not for the primacy of mind,
but for a partnership between the mind and the external
world. The mind, he says in *The Prelude*, is

> creator and receiver both,
> Working but in alliance with the works
> Which it beholds.[1]

He does not rest his faith in "intuitions" as "alone
possible or adequate to the majesty of the Truth"—in
fact, he would not have understood what Coleridge was
talking about: his belief is in

> the discerning intellect of Man,
> When wedded to this goodly universe
> In love and holy passion. . . .[2]

Consistently with this, he regards the senses as
exercising a mediatory function between man and
nature. Hence his reference, in *Tintern Abbey* to "what
they half create, And what perceive".

Coleridge misinterprets Wordsworth's opinions
regarding the mind, the senses, and the external world.
He even forgets that Wordsworth had no philosophical
point of view at all, in the sense in which he here

---

[1] Bk. II. 273.   [2] Preface to *The Excursion*.

demands one of him. His feeling for the history of ideas led Coleridge to look upon eighteenth-century philosophy as moving inevitably towards Humeian scepticism; but Wordsworth, lacking both Coleridge's sense of history and his intellectual finesse, could not see things thus clearly: he was unselfconsciously living the pattern of ideas within which he had grown up.

Wordsworthian criticism is still suffering from this careless identification of attitudes, particularly in respect of his theory of poetry and of the imagination. It is very generally supposed that Wordsworth derived his opinions from Coleridge, and that he derived them ill, because viewed from the standpoint of Coleridge's own theory, they are largely unintelligible.

Poet, for Coleridge, meant Maker. In the tradition of Renaissance Platonism, he thought of the poet not as imitator of the world of appearance, but as creator of a better, because a truer, world. "Her world is brazen, the poets only deliver a golden": Coleridge elaborates Sidney's argument in one of his finest letters:

> The common end of all *narrative*, nay, of *all* Poems, is to convert a *series* into a *Whole*: to make those events, which in real or imagined History move on in a *strait* line, assume to our Understandings a *circular* motion—the snake with its tail in its mouth. Hence indeed the almost flattering and yet appropriate term—Poesy—i.e. poiesis=*making*. Doubtless, to His eye, which alone comprehends all Past and all Future in one eternal Present, what to our short sight appears strait is but a part of the great Cycle—just as the calm sea to us *appears* level, though it be indeed only a part of a *Globe*. Now what the Globe is in Geography, *miniaturing* in order to *manifest* the truth, such is a poem to that image of God, which we were created with. . . .[1]

Kubla Khan is a more compelling statement of the same conviction. The theme of creation with which the

[1] *Unpublished Letters of S. T. Coleridge* (ed. E. L. Griggs), Vol. II. p. 128.

poem opens becomes, in the frenzy of its ending, specifically poetic:

> Could I revive within me
> Her symphony and song,
> To such a deep delight 'twould win me,
> That with music loud and long,
> I would build that dome in air,
> That sunny dome. . . .

And Coleridge's theory of imagination, the "dim analogue of creation", is best understood as a rather forlorn commentary upon *Kubla Khan;* as an attempt to establish discursively that the poet does indeed deliver his golden world and build his dome in air.

For Wordsworth, Poet meant Observer. His theory, and, as he at least believed, his practice, were founded on an assumption inherited by the eighteenth century from Dryden and Ben Jonson, and from classical French criticism, to the effect that poetry is in some sense an imitation of nature. Wordsworth's condemnation of Macpherson's Ossian is typical: "From what I saw with my own eyes, I knew that the imagery was spurious."[1] The picture is such a poor likeness that it must be judged a fake.

This attitude is saved from obvious absurdity by Wordsworth's reliance on the refining and selective power of memory, and by the way he makes the poet's clearsightedness depend upon a disciplined shedding of artifice. Moreover, there is a serious discussion of its linguistic implications in the Preface to the 1815 edition of his poems. When he read this Preface, Coleridge told Byron[2] that it disclosed a wide difference of opinion between Wordsworth and himself as to the nature of the Fancy and the Imagination. Nor is this really surprising; for Coleridge was in complete earnest

[1] See p. 34.
[2] *Unpublished Letters* (ed. E. L. Griggs), Vol. II. p. 143.

about the creative function of the imagination, but had
no interest in the Fancy, except as a relic of eighteenth-
century theory; whereas Wordsworth thought of
imaginative work primarily as the discovery of hitherto
unapprehended relations, and argued that the Fancy
was also, in this limited sense, a creative faculty. Hence,
as between Fancy and Imagination, Coleridge accused
Wordsworth of failure to distinguish, and Wordsworth
Coleridge of distinguishing falsely. Coleridge required
a dramatic contrast between mechanical juxtaposition
and organic synthesis—or rather "prothesis"[1]; for he
wanted a word that suggested identity rather than
union, and so, characteristically, he contrived a
monster. Wordsworth sought not contrast but the
development of a received tradition: he wished to say
something further about the faculty which, in open
defiance of Coleridge, he continued to define as "the
aggregative and associative power".[2]

Just as Coleridge's theory of imagination is a commentary on *Kubla Khan*, so is Wordsworth's a commentary on *The Recluse*,[3] on the fitting of the mind to
the external world, and of the external world to the
mind. The parenthetical line, "theme this but little
heard of among men", indicates that Wordsworth
believed the peculiar significance of *The Recluse* to lie
in its raising of the external world into active and equal
partnership with the mind. His treatment of the
imagination in the 1815 Preface supports the same
conclusion. The whole Preface illuminates Wordsworth's thinking about language and truth; and is
immediately relevant in its concern with careful
observation as the means of achieving a state of action
and reaction between observer and observed. The mind,
regarding objects, and "taking advantage of their appearance to the senses", endows them with properties

[1] J. H. Muirhead, *Coleridge as Philosopher*, p. 87 n.
[2] Preface to the Edition of 1815.   [3] See p. 41.

that do not inhere in them, upon an incitement from properties and qualities the existence of which is inherent and
obvious. These processes of imagination are carried on either
by conferring additional properties upon an object, or
abstracting from it some of those which it actually possesses,
and thus enabling it to re-act upon the mind which hath
performed the process, like a new existence.

Wordsworth's 1815 Preface opens, in the very
manner of an eighteenth-century treatise, with a
solemn account of "the powers requisite for the pro-
duction of poetry", under the headings of Observation
and Description, Sensibility, Reflexion, Imagination
and Fancy, Invention, and Judgment; the which is
followed by a catalogue of Kinds of Poetry: Narrative,
Dramatic, Lyrical, The Idyllium, Didactic, and Philosophical Satire. The background to Wordsworth's
thinking about poetry could not be more clearly indi-
cated; and much of what he has to say only makes
sense when held against it. In the Preface to the
Lyrical Ballads, he states that poetry is in the purest
and profoundest sense scientific. "Poetry is the breath
and finer spirit of all knowledge; it is the impassioned
expression which is in the countenance of all Science."
This is not mere rant: it is the necessary consequence
of his view of the poet as most faithful among students
of appearance. But it *is* appearance that the poet studies.
Wordsworth had little patience with any objective
metaphysic of imagination:

> Imagination is a subjective term: it deals with objects not
> as they are, but as they appear to the mind of the poet.[1]

Coleridge refused to allow that philosophy can end
in the opposition of subject and object. He therefore
abandoned Locke and Hartley for Spinoza. But
Spinoza was only able to overcome this opposition by

[1] Grosart, Vol. III. p. 464.

sacrificing personality: "did philosophy start with an 'it is' instead of an 'I am' Spinoza would be altogether true".[1] So Coleridge left Spinoza, and eventually found other masters. At the same time he saw that neither Wordsworth's acceptance, nor his own rejection, of the condition of subject standing over against a world of objects was a purely intellectual matter: in fact, he achieved clearer understanding of Wordsworth's instinct to draw back and distance his object than did Wordsworth of Coleridge's desire for union. In his *Hymn before Sunrise in the Vale of Chamouny*, Coleridge addresses Mont Blanc thus:

> Thou, the meantime, wast blending with my Thought,
> Yea with my Life, and Life's own secret joy:
> Till the dilating soul, enrapt, transfused,
> Into the mighty vision passing—there
> As in her natural form, swelled vast to Heaven.

And in a letter he records Wordsworth's criticism of these lines:

> Mr Wordsworth, I remember, censured the passage as strained and unnatural, and condemned the Hymn *in toto* (which nevertheless I ventured to publish in the *Sibylline Leaves*) as a specimen of the Mock Sublime. It may be so for others, but it is impossible that I should find it myself unnatural. . . . For from my very childhood I have been accustomed to *abstract* and as it were unrealize whatever of more than common interest my eyes dwelt on; and then by a sort of transference and transmission of my consciousness to identify myself with the Object. . . .[2]

But Wordsworth does not experience this urge towards identity. Even at his most visionary, as when in *Tintern Abbey* he speaks of

> A motion and a spirit that impels
> All thinking things, all objects of all thought,

---

[1] J. H. Muirhead, *Coleridge as Philosopher*, p. 47.
[2] *Unpublished Letters* (ed. E. L. Griggs), Vol. II. p. 261.

the instinct to place the thinking subject on his one hand and the object of his thought on the other does not desert him.

It will be remembered that Coleridge related Wordsworth's natural solitude to the fact that he was "all man".[1] Shelley, noticing the almost complete absence of the erotic in Wordsworth's verse, described him, in *Peter Bell the Third*, as "solemn and unsexual". But Coleridge's suggestion of a withdrawn and brooding masculinity is more profound, for it reckons not only with the absence of erotic,[2] but with Wordsworth's strange attachment at remove, which has a formalized sexual expression in the profuse family images of his poetry. Parent and child metaphors, brotherhood and sisterhood metaphors, household metaphors, are all abundant; and a remarkable number of his important poems have family themes—there is of course *The Brothers;* and also father and son in *Michael;* brother, sister and father, in *The White Doe;* father and daughter in *The Borderers;* mother and child in *The Prelude,* and at other decisive turns in his work. For Wordsworth the family is the universe in microcosm, a complex of individuals related in their independence. The totality which is the family is reflected in his attitude to his brother's death: "God keep the rest of us together! The set is now broken."[3] And again: "as the number of us is now broken, some more of the set will be following him".[4] His is an unusual blend of intelligence and passion; and passion needs emphasis. The certainty of his affection for Dorothy, and of his broken-heartedness at the death of his brother and daughter— the two events that shook his adult life to its founda-

[1] p. 29.
[2] Mr G. Wilson Knight (*The Starlit Dome,* p. 55) contrasts Wordsworth and Shelley in their use of "naked". In Wordsworth, "naked" is without erotic suggestion.
[3] *Early Letters* (ed. de Selincourt), p. 446.
[4] *Ibid.,* p. 476.

tions—is worth an infinity of speculation as to Wordsworth's feelings towards Annette Vallon.

Instead of dismissing Wordsworth as a sexless
phenomenon, Coleridge distinguishes between love,[1]
as the desire for union with the beloved and therefore
able to comprehend only one object, and "long and
deep affection", not necessarily less passionate than
love, expressing itself as an "habitual attachment which
may include many objects". Wordsworth, he argues,
can experience only the latter: "thus Wordsworth is
by nature incapable of being in love, though no man
more tenderly attached". More than this it would be
difficult to say, without building a tendentious thesis
upon the undoubted oddness of Wordsworth's
sexuality.

Solitude and attachment, the huge abstractions
moving through Wordsworth's life and poetry, are in
time joined by his Christianity, which makes its
presence felt in opposition to them. After explaining
that *The Excursion* had disappointed his hope of a poetic
treatment of the Fall and the Redemption, Coleridge
reaffirms that Wordsworth had a greater philosophical
talent than any English poet since Milton, and states
the following reason for his failure to exploit his gifts:

> it seems to me that he ought never to have abandoned the
> contemplative position, which is peculiarly—perhaps I might
> say exclusively—fitted for him. His proper title is *Spectator
> ab extra*.[2]

There is a fundamental confusion here. *The Excursion*
is weaker than *The Prelude* because it lacks the relational and monistic coherence of the earlier poem:
Coleridge has good reason to complain that *The
Prelude's* imaginative strongholds have been surrendered. But Wordsworth has not capriciously

---

[1] *Unpublished Letters* (ed. E. L. Griggs), Vol. II. p. 46.
[2] *Table Talk*, July 31, 1832.

decided to put off him his proper title. He is trying to
write a Christian poem; and Coleridge has failed to see
that the birth of Christianity and the dying of attach-
ment-in-solitude are inseparable issues.

Christianity reached Wordsworth neither through a
sense of sin nor a sense of glory, but through wanhope,
a colourless despair. As he begins *The Prelude*, he says:

> gleams of light
> Flash often from the East, then disappear
> And mock me with a sky that ripens not
> Into a steady morning. . . .[1]

Coleridge rightly insists on Wordsworth's extreme
masculinity: he is a striking exception to the classical
type of bi-sexual genius; and there is from the start
something incomplete about his "self-sufficing power
of solitude". Hence the restlessness of the early
Prelude:

> the soul
> Remembering how she felt, but what she felt
> Remembering not, retains an obscure sense
> Of possible sublimity, to which
> With growing faculties she doth aspire,
> With faculties still growing, feeling still
> That whatsoever point they gain, they still
> Have something to pursue.[2]

And even the spiritual triumph which he experienced
upon crossing the Alps dwells upon potentiality rather
than present possession:

> in such visitings
> Of awful promise, when the light of sense
> Goes out in flashes that have shown to us
> The invisible world, doth Greatness make abode,
> There harbours whether we be young or old.

[1] Bk. I. 134.   [2] Bk. II. 334.

> Our destiny, our nature, and our home
> Is with infinitude, and only there;
> With hope it is, hope that can never die,
> Effort, and expectation, and desire,
> And something evermore about to be.[1]

Wordsworth's sense of "possible sublimity" sustained the terrible, vague urgency of this struggle from partial vision to partial vision. When he lost that sense, he ceased to tread "the very edge of vacancy". And this is more than failure of nerve, for the will is of very limited importance in the total involvement of the *Prelude* experience.

Wordsworth refers his great loss to two causes. The first, the gradual dulling of sensibility in the face of the natural world, is one of the themes of the Immortality Ode, and is hinted at in *The Prelude* itself:

> The days gone by
> Come back upon me from the dawn almost
> Of life: the hiding-places of my power
> Seem open; I approach, and then they close;
> I see by glimpses now; when age comes on,
> May scarcely see at all. . . .[2]

The second is a sudden accident. In February 1805, Wordsworth received news of his brother's death in shipwreck; and later in the same year he wrote his *Elegiac Stanzas suggested by a Picture of Peele Castle in a Storm*. Wordsworth recounts that he once lived within sight of Peele Castle during a long period of fine weather, so that had he then painted the castle, his picture would have been very different from that other which occasioned his poem:

> Ah! THEN, if mine had been the Painter's hand,
> To express what then I saw; and add the gleam,
> The light that never was, on sea or land,
> The consecration, and the Poet's dream;

[1] Bk. VI. 533.   [2] Bk. XI. 334.

> I would have painted thee, thou hoary Pile
> Amid a world how different from this!
> Beside a sea that could not cease to smile;
> On tranquil land, beneath a sky of bliss.

But such a picture is no longer possible:

> Not for a moment now could I behold
> A smiling sea, and be what I have been:
> The feeling of my loss will ne'er be old;
> This, which I know, I speak with mind serene.

His brother's death had brought about a universal change:

> So once it would have been—'tis now no more;
> I have submitted to a new control:
> A power is gone, which nothing can restore;
> A deep distress hath humanized my Soul.

It has destroyed his "sense of possible sublimity", or, in the present lovely paraphrase, it has quenched

> the gleam,
> The light that never was, on sea or land,
> The consecration, and the Poet's dream.

Wordsworth describes his crisis as an abandonment of solitude, thus inadvertently confirming Coleridge's statement of his case:

> Farewell, farewell the heart that lives alone,
> Housed in a dream, at distance from the Kind!

And in the place of solitude he speaks of a new humanity, and a "mind serene". This is a very large issue. Immediately, it touches the Stoicism of Wordsworth's middle years, the Roman severity foreshadowed in the final stanza:

> But welcome fortitude, and patient cheer,
> And frequent sights of what is to be borne!

And ultimately it concerns Wordsworth's Christianity.

John Wordsworth's death set his brother to much heart-searching:

> A thousand times have I asked myself, as your tender sympathy led me to do, "why was he taken away?" and I have answered the question as you have done. In fact there is no other answer that can satisfy and lay the mind at rest. Why have we a choice and a will, and a notion of justice and injustice, enabling us to be moral agents? Why have we sympathies that make the best of us so afraid of inflicting pain and sorrow, which yet we see dealt about so lavishly by the supreme governor? Why should our notions of right towards each other, and to all sentient beings within our influence, differ so widely from what appears to be His notion and rule, if everything were to end here? Would it not be blasphemy to say that, upon the supposition of the thinking principle being destroyed by death, however inferior we may be to the great Cause and Ruler of things, we have *more of love* in our nature than he has? The thought is monstrous; and yet how to get rid of it, except on the supposition of *another* and a *better world*, I do not see.[1]

Wordsworth does not embrace Christianity: it is forced on him by the exclusion of alternatives. His admission, almost reluctant, that there must be "another and a better world" is followed by regular Christian observance; and this, I shall attempt to show, by a late and Christian maturity. He was still writing *The Prelude* when his brother died; his effort was directed elsewhere, and the first steps were taken with much hesitation. He was at all times a stubborn man, and, as Shelley said,

> he never could
> Fancy another situation,
> From which to dart his contemplation,
> Than that wherein he stood.[2]

---

[1] *Early Letters* (ed. de Selincourt), p. 460.   [2] *Peter Bell the Third.*

His masculinity is again pertinent. Only towards the end of a very long life did he achieve that condition of spirit, perhaps essentially feminine, in which intellectual paradox is resolved, and not merely opposed, in faith.

Important also is his blindness to sin: the most direct way to a Christian understanding of suffering was thereby closed to him; and he was left to follow a much longer path, determined by recurring patterns of ceremonial, by the quiet influence of local and ancient pieties, and of catholic association. Invincibly Protestant only in his political hatred of the Roman Church, he grew, in the course of time, into intelligent sympathy with the Tractarian Movement. And he came to look, for his religion's chief support, towards the Incarnation, whereby the duality of earth and Heaven, else to him intolerable, is taken upon unweary shoulders.

Thus I persuade myself that I have seen three things. There is the poetry of solitude and relationship. There is the poetry of indecision, of glances behind and before—the poetry, pre-eminently, of *The Excursion* and *The White Doe*, long works of Wordsworth's middle age. And then, though this has not yet been touched on, there is the offering of a baptized imagination.

II

SOLITUDE AND RELATIONSHIP

WORDSWORTH'S tragedy, *The Borderers*, is the last work assigned by him to the class of "Poems written in Youth". Finished in 1797, and standing at the threshold of the Great Decade, the play has been a good deal noticed. It has been judged the unhappy result of Wordsworth's disillusionment with the French Revolution, or of a rash encounter with Godwin's *Enquiry concerning Political Justice*; and Annette Vallon has been held responsible for its consideration of remorse within a history of crime and punishment. Annette's influence must be a matter of conjecture, indeed of idle conjecture; for even if the thesis of her desertion by Wordsworth and of the gradual stifling of his genius in guilty contemplation of his act be wholly accepted, we still know nothing of his coming to be a poet, or of his achievement in poetry: we have discovered merely a reason for his falling off. Godwin's *Political Justice*, on the other hand, has certainly left its mark upon *The Borderers*, in the form of a plodding intellectualism that makes the play almost unreadable. Time and again the principles of Godwin's philosophy are stubbornly debated:

> I feel
> That you have shown, and by a signal instance,
> How they who would be just must seek the rule
> By diving for it into their own bosoms.
> To-day you have thrown off a tyranny
> That lives but in the torpid acquiescence
> Of the world's masters, with the musty rules
> By which they uphold their craft from age to age:
> You have obeyed the only law that sense

> Submits to recognize; the immediate law,
> From the clear light of circumstances, flashed
> Upon an independent Intellect.[1]

Wordsworth may have been not entirely unaware of his desperate poverty in dramatic talent, for he makes the disarming admission that *The Borderers* was written "without any view to its exhibition upon the stage".[2] This is borne out by a reckless inattention to coherence of plot and consistency of character. No doubt Wordsworth was preoccupied with Godwin. But Godwin is of very transient importance in Wordsworth's poetry, whereas Shakespeare, whose shadow also lies across the play, is not. Wordsworth's parading of the externals of Shakespearean tragedy is merely tiresome: the thing that matters, and, perhaps, the thing that caused Coleridge to overpraise *The Borderers*, is its lively connexion with *Othello*, *Macbeth*, and *King Lear*.

The Borderers is about the doings of a band of philanthropic outlaws in the reign of Henry III. Marmaduke, their leader, is in love with Idonea, who is the joy and sole support of her father, the baron Herbert. Herbert has been cheated of his estates while crusading in Palestine, and wanders, old, blind, and helpless, through the play. Deceived by Oswald, a member of his band, Marmaduke causes the death of Herbert, and so loses Idonea.

Oswald is not a simple villain. Wordsworth refers, in his Preface, to Iago, and the correspondences between the two are clear. Oswald "nourishes a contempt for mankind the more dangerous because he has been led to it by reflection".[3] He regards "the world as a body which is in some sort of war with him"[4]; and this, coupled with a huge pride and love of power, leads him

---

[1] *l.* 1484.   [2] Note to *The Borderers*.
[3] *P.W.*, Vol. I. p. 346.   [4] *Ibid.*, p. 346.

E

to a course of action purely destructive and indulged for its own sake. His character is a study in "the apparently *motiveless* actions of bad men"[1]; and Wordsworth, faithful to the spirit of Iago, draws him passionless and cynically regardant:

> *Idonea.*   . . . if erring,
>   Oh let me be forgiven!
> *Marmaduke.* I *do* forgive thee.
> *Id.* But take me to your arms—this breast, alas!
>   It throbs, and you have a heart that does not feel it.
> *Marm (exultingly).* She is innocent. [*He embraces her.*
> *Oswald (aside).*   Were I a Moralist
>   I should make wondrous revolution here;
>   It were a quaint experiment to show
>   The beauty of truth. . . .[2]

Oswald raises the question not only of apparently motiveless wrongdoing, but of perseverence in crime. Wordsworth's Preface states it thus:

> We all know that the dissatisfaction accompanying the first impulses towards a criminal action, where the mind is familiar with guilt, acts as a stimulus to proceed in that action. . . . Besides, in a course of criminal conduct every fresh step that we make appears a justification of the one which preceded it, it seems to bring again the moment of liberty and choice; it banishes the idea of repentance, and seems to set remorse at defiance.[3]

Here Wordsworth turns to *Macbeth*, and into Oswald's character he works a distinct trace of the frantic hero, seeking action of any kind as a relief from guilty thoughts, and holding converse with Spirits. The scene of Oswald's incitement of Marmaduke to the murder is heavy with *Macbeth*. Marmaduke is unable to kill Herbert because he resembles Idonea in his sleep, and Oswald waits until Marmaduke "comes forth with

---

[1] *P.W.*, Vol. I. p. 343.   [2] *l.* 1617.   [3] *P.W.*, Vol. I. p. 347.

bloody hands",[1] arguing, in the version finished in
1797, that "a little water clears us of this deed":

> In the torrent hard by there is water enough
> to wash away all the blood in the universe.[2]

As in *Macbeth*, the image of bloody hands returns much
later in the play:

> Here is my hand—The hue of a pure lily,
> A Lady hand—none of your crimson spots.[3]

The presence of *Lear* is much more strongly felt.
Herbert, "meek and patient, feeble, old and blind",
moves in the likeness of Shakespeare's king, against a
background of desolation, storm, and human violence.
Dispossessed and exposed in utter helplessness, he is
Lear's realization of bare humanity; he is the "forked
animal", the "thing itself". And beyond this affinity
between characters there is the full savagery of setting:

> The storm beats hard—Mercy for poor or rich
> Whose heads are shelterless in such a night![4]

> We should deserve to wear a cap and bells
> Three good round years, for playing the fool here
> In such a night as this.[5]

> Howl, howl, poor dog! Thou'lt never find him more;
> Draggled with storm and wet, howl, howl amain. . . .[6]

> . . . perhaps
> He is not in his true and perfect mind.[7]

The Borderers recovers something of *Lear's* giant
perplexity in the face of the primary forms of things;
of naked suffering and endurance ranged against the

[1] *l.* 938.
[3] *Ibid.*, p. 221.
[5] *l.* 768.
[7] *Ibid.*, p. 353.

[2] *P.W.*, Vol. I. p. 166.
[4] *l.* 1882.
[6] *P.W.*, Vol. I. p. 220.

elemental cruelties of neighbour and neighbourhood. Lear's all-embracing bewilderment is echoed here:

> I am perplexed, and cannot think it true
> That thus thou speak'st to me, and where I am
> I know not, nor if this be the same air
> And the same sun, and we are fellow beings,
> Or all is changed. . . .[1]

As between Lear and Cordelia, so between Herbert and Idonea, there is the suggestion, in the midst of pain, of a golden other-life of prayer and song:

> There is a psalm that speaks
> Of God's parental mercies—with Idonea
> I used to sing it.[2]

And Wordsworth, like Shakespeare, throws out abrupt statements of vast and hazy significance, about maturity, and patience, and the cyclical nature of things:

> The dead have but one face. . . .[3]

> . . . . the grave
> Contains not all that perish. . . .[4]

> So meet extremes in this mysterious world. . . .[5]

But because they have not the massive structure of *Lear* behind them, they sound in their context ghostly thin. Herbert is a pale character, a mere sufferer, and such strength as *The Borderers* possesses is not bent towards his dying. In a scene which he later omitted, but which contains the best verse of the play, Wordsworth introduces a Pilgrim who is a study in miniature of Herbert, conforming perfectly to the type of lonely and agonized wanderer. Those who watch as he passes

---

[1] *P.W.*, Vol. I. p. 355.
[2] l. 1266.
[3] l. 2162.
[4] *P.W.*, Vol. I. p. 356.
[5] l. 1529.

by, try to tempt him from his destiny by offering as an
alternative life a curious blend of Christian sanctity and
pastoral sweetness:

> A holy man,
> We know you are heaven-favoured; freshest grass
> Shall strew your chamber and a candlestick
> And crucifix with picture of the virgin
> Stand at the right hand of your humble bed,
> And you shall feed my sheep, and the long day
> Their quiet shall be yours.[1]

But the Pilgrim, "on whose brow affliction's hand had
left So little of earthly", rejects this resolution and
proceeds on his way.

In the last two Acts of *The Borderers*, Wordsworth
dwells upon the contrasted solitudes of Oswald and
Marmaduke. Oswald, the Godwinian apologist, is set
against the world by his individualistic rationalism.
Rejecting traditional moralities, and holding "that
merit has no surer test Than obloquy", he describes
himself as "sounding on, Through words and things, a
dim and perilous way".[2] Wordsworth repeats this
phrase in *The Excursion*, with specific reference to
intellect:

> By pain of heart—now checked—and now impelled—
> The intellectual power, through words and things,
> Went sounding on, a dim and perilous way![3]

And the isolation of intellectual genius is very well
stated in *The Prelude* lines on Newton's statue:

> The marble index of a mind for ever
> Voyaging through strange seas of Thought, alone.[4]

Oswald has no successors, because Wordsworth's
concern with the solitude of reason does not survive his

---

[1] *P.W.*, Vol. I. p. 354.   [2] l. 1774.
[3] Bk. III. 699.   [4] 1850, Bk. III. 62.

loss of interest in Godwin. Marmaduke, on the other
hand, takes upon himself at the end of the play the
mantle of Herbert and the Pilgrim: he accepts his
solitude as a condition imposed by the natural order of
things, uncontrived and inescapable. This larger solitude dominates Wordsworth's poetry for the next ten
years.

> No prayers, no tears, but hear my doom in silence.
> I will go forth a wanderer on the earth,
> A shadowy thing, and as I wander on
> No human ear shall ever hear me speak,
> No human dwelling ever give me food
> Or sleep or rest, and all the uncertain way
> Shall be as darkness to me, as a waste
> Unnamed by man![1]

As he sets out on his lonely course, Marmaduke asks
why men should ever seek each other, even in
extremity:

> Give me a reason why the wisest thing
> That the earth owns should never choose to die,
> But some one must be near to count his groans.
> The wounded deer retires to solitude,
> And dies in solitude: all things but man,
> All die in solitude.[2]

Wordsworth's hasty sketches in solitude are inspired
by the bleakness of *Lear*, by its preoccupation with the
elements of things natural and human ("Then let them
anatomize Regan. . . ." "What is the cause of
thunder?"), by the stumbling figure of the king.
Regan tells her father: "Nature in you stands at the

---

[1] *P.W.*, Vol. I. p. 224. When he revised *The Borderers* in 1842 Wordsworth made Marmaduke wander abroad "in search of nothing, that this
earth can give, But expiation" (ll. 2317-8). The idea of expiation is foreign
to his original conception of the play.
[2] l. 2149.

very verge of her confine"; and for Wordsworth the total isolation of Lear ruined—forsaken, dispossessed, lunatic, immeasurably old—is the play's heart. In the final scenes of *Lear*, Shakespeare achieves the co-presence of great suffering and of a state beyond suffering, a state of peace embodied but not conceptualized, a substance walking shadowless upon the stage. Wordsworth also, at the end of *The Borderers*, points in suffering beyond suffering. Marmaduke is

> raised
> Above or sunk below, all further sense
> Of provocation.[1]

He counsels Idonea:

> Conflict must cease, and in thy frozen heart,
> The extremes of suffering meet in absolute peace.[2]

Both plays look beyond pain; but what is said slantingly and with the terrible weight of *Lear* behind it, becomes in *The Borderers* ineffectually direct. Wordsworth fails because he asks last questions first: he understands reconcilement in solitude, but he cannot present a world broken on the wheel. And it is impossible to believe in Wordsworth's resolution without first believing in his tragedy.

Wordsworth learnt from his failure in *The Borderers*. He did not attempt another play: he came, in fact, to see that his talent was not only undramatic in its kind, but in a positive sense the denial of drama. All his solitaries of the next few years are in their different ways at peace with their environment; and although they live on the other side of tragedy, there is no attempt to derive their situation from tragic conflict—they have always been where Wordsworth finds them,

[1] l. 2294.   [2] l. 2215.

and they remain there after he has gone. So it is with the Old Cumberland Beggar:

> Him from my childhood have I known; and then
> He was so old, he seems not older now;
> He travels on, a solitary man. . . .

And with the Leech-Gatherer:

> In my mind's eye I seemed to see him pace
> About the weary moors continually,
> Wandering about alone and silently.[1]

The impression is of eternal lonely wandering at a slow and even pace, and through a single boundless element. Silence is also important. Wordsworth's solitaries are often wholly inarticulate, like the Cumberland Beggar, or half articulate, with a mysterious private utterance, like the Discharged Soldier in *The Prelude:*

> From his lips meanwhile
> There issued murmuring sounds, as if of pain
> Or of uneasy thought . . . he remained
> Fix'd in his place, and still from time to time
> Sent forth a murmuring voice of dead complaint,
> Groans scarcely audible.[2]

Almost none of the Leech-Gatherer's conversation is reported in his own words, and so it does not obtrude itself upon the poem. By avoiding direct speech Wordsworth is able to indicate a power to overreach, in the Leech-Gatherer's presence, the huge dualism of word and voice, language and action:

> The old Man still stood talking by my side;
> But now his voice to me was like a stream
> Scarce heard; nor word from word could I divide;
> And the whole body of the Man did seem
> Like one whom I had met with in a dream;
> Or like a man from some far region sent,
> To give me human strength, by apt admonishment.

---

[1] *Resolution and Independence.*   [2] Bk. IV. 421.

In the first published version of *Old Man Travelling*, a poem short enough to quote in full, Wordsworth presents a solitary who is straightforwardly articulate:

> The little hedgerow birds,
> That peck along the road regard him not.
> He travels on, and in his face, his step,
> His gait, is one expression: every limb,
> His look and bending figure, all bespeak
> A man who does not move with pain, but moves
> With thought—He is insensibly subdued
> To settled quiet: he is one by whom
> All effort seems forgotten; one to whom
> Long patience hath such mild composure given,
> That patience now doth seem a thing of which
> He hath no need. He is by nature led
> To peace so perfect that the young behold
> With envy, what the Old Man hardly feels.
> —I asked him whither he was bound, and what
> The object of his journey; he replied
> "Sir! I am going many miles to take
> A last leave of my son, a mariner,
> Who from a sea-fight hath been brought to Falmouth,
> And there is dying in a hospital.[1]

Later, Wordsworth saw that the last six lines were a mistake, and he saved the poem by omitting them. The point is not that they are trite or prosaic, but that they do violence to the nature of the old man. Just as Wordsworth is admonished by "the whole body" of the Leech-Gatherer, of which his stream-like voice is one constituent, even so does the total aspect of the old man perfectly "bespeak" his condition. He does not need to do or say anything—he is. Like all the great solitaries, he has a primordial quality by virtue of which he stands anterior, in time or in logic, to a divorce in human understanding. Saying and doing, with all of

[1] *P.W.*, Vol. IV. p. 247.

them, are contained in what they are. Wordsworth tries
to touch this mystery, in a comment on an early version
of *The Leech-Gatherer:*

> A person reading this Poem with feelings like mine will
> have been awed and controuled, expecting almost something
> spiritual or supernatural—What is brought forward? "A
> lonely place, a Pond" "by which an old man *was*, far from
> all house or home"—not stood, not sat, but *"was"*—the
> figure presented in the most naked simplicity possible.[1]

Wordsworth's use of the verb "to be" in the poetry
of this period is directly related, as he says, to the
simplicity of his solitaries, which is as large as it is
naked. By this means he calls upon the vast and the
remote without reference to space, and upon the old
and the enduring without reference to time. "To be",
in Wordsworth, is the agent of primary meaning, not
pointing forward in argument towards *ex post facto*
synthesis, but bending back, like the growing child in
the Immortality Ode, upon an entire experience. Under
its influence,

> Our souls have sight of that immortal sea
> That brought us hither. . . .

In order to make one word do so much work, Wordsworth, like Humpty Dumpty, has to pay it extra. How
hard it works we discover when we find ourselves, as
we talk about these solitaries, groping among inert
abstractions. Wordsworth does this himself. His alternative title for *Old Man Travelling* is *Animal Tranquillity and Decay*. *The Leech-Gatherer*, of course, is
properly called *Resolution and Independence*, and in a
letter about the poem Wordsworth contemplates "the
fortitude, independence, persevering spirit, and the
general moral dignity of this old man's character".[2]
This is no substitute for the Leech-Gatherer, who is

---

[1] *Early Letters* (ed. de Selincourt), p. 306.
[2] *Ibid.*, p. 306.

what he is; and the question, "what is he?", can only be answered by the poem.

Convinced of the uniqueness of the poetic activity and of its power to comprehend experience, Words-worth said some wild things about language and reality. No poet has ever complained so much as he about the medium of his art; and towards the close of the Great Decade this complaint comes to wear a sinister aspect. Repeatedly, and with a helpless shrug, Wordsworth deplores the inadequacies of language: he says, of those whom he places highest among men:

> Words are but under-agents in their souls;
> When they are grasping with their greatest strength
> They do not breathe among them. . . .[1]

These are signs of his flinching from poetry. But his earlier dissatisfaction is not with language as in its nature unable to meet his demands upon it, but with the failure of himself and others before him to exploit its full resources.

According to the Preface to the *Lyrical Ballads*, poetry ought to be "the image of man and nature"; and in working towards this ideal, it appeals to the language of rustic and humble life, as to a perfect model. Even the language of the greatest poets

> must often, in liveliness and truth, fall short of that which is uttered by men in real life, under the actual pressure of those passions, certain shadows of which the Poet thus produces, or feels to be produced, in himself.

Inept in argument and conventional in expression, the Preface reveals that conspiracy of faculties without which great poetry has not been written. The possible perfection towards which its theory is directed is not the perfection of an autonomous linguistic world, a treadmill from which no poet can escape, in success or in failure, in abuse of poetic diction or in praise of

[1] *The Prelude*, Bk. XII. 272.

silence. Rather, it is an inclusive perfection, admitting no distinction between language and not-language. Language is an effective inhabitant of all possible worlds; it can "deal boldly with substantial things"; it can encompass the human predicament and make plain "what we are". "Is there not", Wordsworth asks in *The Recluse*, "a strain of words that shall be life?" At the time he started work on *The Recluse* and wrote the *Lyrical Ballads* Preface, the question was rhetorical. A refusal to allow any final separation of language and life lies behind his confused discussion of the poet's duty of fidelity to fact, and of his moral and scientific status. His entire devotion to poetry, and readiness to risk all in its profession, would otherwise have been impossible.

The Leech-Gatherer, "the whole body of the man", is presented in terms of an integration which, in the strength of the poem, is defined into neither synthesis nor identity: he is like a cloud, says Wordsworth, that "moveth all together, if it move at all". The point of focus of this integration is the eloquence by which Wordsworth is admonished, containing, as it does, the rival eloquencies of sound and sight. *Old Man Travelling* is also a study in integration, but of a different kind. The poem may be approached as a Cartesian essay on the relationship of thing and thought. On his journey, the old man keeps the company of abstractions: "in his face, his step, his gait, is one expression"; he is "a man who does not move with pain, but moves with thought"; he is "subdued to settled quiet"; "patience" has given him "mild composure"; he is led "to peace". In all this intercourse neither his nor their nature is denied: he is an old man, yet not reified into mere particularity, while they retain their universality in the poem, although strangely breathed upon. It is the power of Wordsworth's Roman imagination to move between abstract and concrete in a way that is now lost to men: he would have understood words like *mens* and *fides* which look to us sometimes like ordinary abstract nouns and sometimes like personifications.

In the large simplicity of these solitaries, the difference becomes clear which Wordsworth struggled to express in prose, between the thing poetically distinct and the thing reduced to singleness.[1] They earn their independence by their show of comprehension, of relational power; and this independence is accepted as genuine because it is not achieved at the expense of experienced differences, as, in the two cases just considered, of that between language and action and between thought and thing.

Their isolation has its external aspect, which Wordsworth states immediately. All of them are placed at the verge of life; in earliest childhood or extreme old age, in dispossession, in unemployment or in utter poverty, in lunacy or blindness, in pursuit of the lonely callings of mendicant or pedlar. The further consequences of their solitude are then made plain. Just as they are wanderers through space, so are they gatherers up of time. The Cumberland Beggar, "in that vast solitude to which The tide of things has borne him", seems no older than he did when Wordsworth first met him: his solitude is no less temporal than spatial. Of another solitary Wordsworth says that he had an eye

> that, under brows
> Shaggy and grey, had meanings which it brought
> From years of youth; which, like a Being made
> Of many Beings, he had wondrous skill
> To blend with knowledge of the years to come,
> Human, or such as lie beyond the grave.[2]

[1] See p. 34.
[2] *The Excursion*, Bk. I. 428. The passage is early, belonging to 1797, the year of *The Old Cumberland Beggar*. See *P.W.*, Vol. V. p. 387.

This encompassing of all modes of being, and of the conditions of life and death and sleep, is perfectly established in *The Leech-Gatherer:*

> As a huge stone is sometimes seen to lie
> Couched on the bald top of an eminence;
> Wonder to all who do the same espy,
> By what means it could thither come, and whence;
> So that it seemed a thing endued with sense:
> Like a sea-beast crawled forth, that on a shelf
> Of rock or sand reposeth, there to sun itself;
>
> Such seemed this Man, not all alive nor dead,
> Nor all asleep—in his extreme old age. . . .

These figures do not achieve their sovereign peace through any vulgar triumph of permanence over process. The Cumberland Beggar, in his vast solitude, still pursues the endless circuit of houses, in search of alms; and the Leech-Gatherer will always pace "about the weary moors", plying his trade from pool to pool. They understand, and this is a key to their true independence, that only the permanent can change. They have a stillness which does not deny movement, and movement which contains stillness; the whole self-sustaining in a final and heroic shedding of accident that foreshadows *The Excursion*'s

> Authentic tidings of invisible things;
> Of ebb and flow, and everduring power;
> And central peace, subsisting at the heart
> Of endless agitation.[1]

The old man is consumed with the effort of his journey; yet "he is one to whom All effort seems forgotten". The discharged soldier[2] arrests Wordsworth with his "groans scarcely audible" and with "the ghastly mildness in his look"; but Wordsworth discovers that "in all he said There was a strange half-absence", and that

[1] Bk. IV. 1144.   [2] See p. 62.

he speaks in the tone of one "Remembering the importance of his theme But feeling it no longer". The soldier is at peace, and he is fully acquainted with suffering. Here Wordsworth succeeds, where in *The Borderers* he failed, in penetrating to the other side of pain. There is no shirking the desperate personal issue: the soldier's personality is real, and so is his distress:

> He was of stature tall,
> A foot above man's common measure tall,
> Stiff in his form, and upright, lank and lean;
> A man more meagre, as it seem'd to me,
> Was never seen abroad by night or day.
> His arms were long, and bare his hands; his mouth
> Shew'd ghastly in the moonlight: from behind
> A milestone propp'd him, and his figure seem'd
> Half-sitting, and half-standing. I could mark
> That he was clad in military garb,
> Though faded, yet entire. He was alone,
> Had no attendant, neither Dog, nor Staff,
> Nor knapsack; in his very dress appear'd
> A desolation, a simplicity
> That seem'd akin to solitude.

And his immediate need of "food and lodgings for the night" is plainly stated. But somehow he has reached, through war, a peace that is not dependent upon the exclusion of strife, upon insensibility or oblivion.

We should be guided by Wordsworth's understanding of externals. The soldier is fully human, yet marvellously tall, and "ghastly in the moonlight". He is in the world, yet placed "half-sitting and half-standing", between the worlds. His soldier's dress, "though faded, yet entire". The last stroke is the most subtle. Nothing is lost to the soldier, but everything is changed: he is history at last become wholly meaningful. Thus when, after sustained concrete description, Wordsworth turns to three of his favourite abstractions

—"desolation", "simplicity", "solitude"—they are ready to work very hard for him.

The soldier's faded uniform is beautifully relevant to his story of violence and death, which he tells like one "Remembering the importance of his theme But feeling it no longer". In his case, the relational power which he shares with the other solitaries is focused on the opposition of war and peace; and the overcoming of this opposition is referred to as an act of memory. Memory, we shall see, is the vital centre of a theory that poetry "takes its origin from emotion recollected in tranquillity":[1] memory distinguishes the visionary soul, described as

> Remembering how she felt, but what she felt
> Remembering not. . . .[2]

Here, memory commands the spiritual totality that is Wordsworthian solitude.

Lucy must also be counted among the solitaries, although clearly different from the others. All the Lucy Poems, with one undistinguished exception,[3] were written in Germany, in the winter of 1798-99. During some of the coldest weather of the century, Wordsworth lodged with his sister in a provincial town, separated from Coleridge, very short of money, disliking the Germans and understanding little of their language. This may have some bearing on the extraordinary quality of the Lucy Poems; on their remoteness, on their clarity and microcosmic perfection. They touch the same issues as Wordsworth's other poetry of solitude and relationship, but their extreme spirituality of tone and lack of literal context is altogether untypical. Even the discharged soldier, the most ghostly

---

[1] Preface to the *Lyrical Ballads*.
[2] *The Prelude*, Bk. II. 335.
[3] *I travelled among unknown men. . . .*

of the relational solitaries, has about him enough of
earthly matter of fact to be judged no ghost.

There are two poems, also written in Germany,
which ought to be included in the Lucy canon. Of
these, *The Danish Boy* is very close to Lucy. He is a
spirit of eternal youth and solitude, in a paradisal
setting:

> Between two sister moorland rills
> There is a spot that seems to lie
> Sacred to flowerets of the hills,
> And sacred to the sky.
> And in this smooth and open dell
> There is a tempest-stricken tree;
> A corner-stone by lightning cut,
> The last stone of a lonely hut;
> And in this dell you see
> A thing no storm can e'er destroy,
> The shadow of a Danish Boy.

This is the highly stylized Lucy setting; and in its
midst,

> The Danish Boy walks here alone:
> This lovely dell is all his own.

He is the maker of music too fine for human ear, the
expression of his perfect sympathy with the life
surrounding him:

> A harp is from his shoulder slung;
> Resting the harp upon his knee,
> To words of a forgotten tongue
> He suits its melody.
> Of flocks upon the neighbouring hill
> He is the darling and the joy;
> And often, when no cause appears,
> The mountain-ponies prick their ears,
> —They hear the Danish Boy.
> While in the dell he sings alone
> Beside the tree and corner-stone.

F

And in the last stanza he holds war and peace, life and death, reconciled in his unearthly song:

> There sits he; in his face you spy
> No trace of a ferocious air,
> Nor ever was a cloudless sky
> So steady or so fair.
> The lovely Danish Boy is blest
> And happy in his flowery cove:
> From bloody deeds his thoughts are far;
> And yet he warbles songs of war,
> That seem like songs of love,
> For calm and gentle is his mien;
> Like a dead Boy he is serene.

Within its tiny compass, this poem succeeds in stating the Lucy theme.

Lucy Gray, the second of the poems outside the recognized canon, introduces in its opening stanzas the classical nature-solitary:

> Oft I had heard of Lucy Gray:
> And, when I crossed the wild,
> I chanced to see at break of day
> The solitary child.
>
> No mate, no comrade Lucy knew;
> She dwelt on the wide moor,
> —The sweetest thing that ever grew
> Beside a human door!

There follows a tale of death in sudden accident: and Lucy Gray finally returns, a singing child-ghost, to haunt the poem:

> —Yet some maintain that to this day
> She is a living child;
> That you may see sweet Lucy Gray
> Upon the lonesome wild.

> O'er rough and smooth she trips along,
> And never looks behind;
> And sings a solitary song
> That whistles in the wind.

The Lucy Poems share this preoccupation with perfect solitude discovered in perfect relationship with environment. *She Dwelt among Untrodden Ways* presents Lucy as a single jewel well set:

> A violet by a mossy stone
> Half hidden from the eye!
> —Fair as a star, when only one
> Is shining in the sky.

And *A Slumber Did My Spirit Seal* imagines her, much more sternly, as joined with the primary forms of nature in eternal cosmic movement:

> Rolled round in earth's Jiurnal course
> With rocks, and stones, and trees.

Of the remaining poems, *Strange Fits of Passion* is brilliantly and obliquely evocative of solitude. Lucy's cottage is the still point round which the poem is constructed; and the poet's journey towards it is described with a Coleridgean sense of foreboding:

> My horse moved on; hoof after hoof
> He raised, and never stopped:
> When down behind the cottage roof,
> At once, the bright moon dropped.

Lucy's ethereal remoteness is enforced by the way the poem ends with the poet still riding towards her cottage, struck by the sudden fear that she may be dead.

Three Years She Grew, the last of the group, considers the relationship between the solitary and her world as a thing of purity and finest eloquence, the

lyrical delicacy of the verse scarcely equalled in Wordsworth:

> The floating clouds their state shall lend
> To her; for her the willow bend;
> Nor shall she fail to see
> Even in the motions of the Storm
> Grace that shall mould the Maiden's form
> By silent sympathy.
>
> The stars of midnight shall be dear
> To her; and she shall lean her ear
> In many a secret place
> Where rivulets dance their wayward round,
> And beauty born of murmuring sound
> Shall pass into her face.

Lucy's beauty is a universal thing, a Wordsworthian
music of the spheres: the music of sight in the first
stanza is joined by the music of sound in the second,
which two beget a greater music that they both must
recognize.

It is thus possible to see the Lucy Poems as consistent both with each other and with the rest of Wordsworth's poetry. There is evident, in everything that
Wordsworth writes, a vision of reality as single, self-
sustaining, and systematic. Hence, I have argued, his
imaginative Spinozism; and, rather as Spinoza thought
it possible, without relapsing into Cartesian dualism,
to consider his Substance either under the aspect of
Thought or of Extension, so Wordsworth moves from
solitude to relationship and back again, without losing
grip upon the fact of singleness. The one may only be
reduced to the other, but the reduction may be perfect.
Wordsworth can talk about Lucy's beauty in solitude,
in the last quotation, only in terms of a relationship
between visual and aural: both are present in her,
because the beauty that "passed into her face" was
"born of murmuring sound". But this, in Words-

worth's lyric, is entirely adequate. Nor does it matter whether Wordsworth's poetry be approached through the one or the other: only the simultaneity of the poetry itself is unattainable. And the bungled studies of solitude in *The Borderers*, leading to success, have their exact counterpart in relationship.

Lucy's "silent sympathy" with nature affords a leading text. This sympathy is the obsession of Wordsworth's juvenile descriptive poetry, and passages like the following from *An Evening Walk*, decked out in the manners of eighteenth-century sentimental reflection, are all too common:

> Last evening sight, the cottage smoke, no more,
> Lost in the thickened darkness, glimmers hoar;
> And, towering from the sullen, dark-brown mere,
> Like a black wall, the mountain-steeps appear.
> —Now o'er the soothed accordant heart we feel
> A sympathetic twilight slowly steal,
> And ever, as we fondly muse, we find
> The soft gloom deepening on the tranquil mind.[1]

At this early stage there is nothing to arrest the attention, beyond Wordsworth's persistence in this theme, and the signs of his serious intellectual application to it. In 1794, the year after he published *An Evening Walk*, Wordsworth was engaged in its amendment. The 1794 corrections are of interest, for they develop a vitalistic philosophy of nature in defence of these repeated assertions of sympathy:

> A heart that vibrates evermore, awake
> To feeling for all forms that Life can take,
> That wider still its sympathy extends
> And sees not any line where being ends;

[1] l. 311. The edition of 1793 (*P.W.*, Vol. I. p. 34) does not differ in any important respect from the shorter final version here quoted.

> Sees sense, through Nature's rudest forms betrayed,
> Tremble obscure through fountain, rock, and shade,
> And while a secret power those forms endears
> Their social accents never vainly hears.[1]

And a few lines later Wordsworth speaks of "those favoured souls" who

> See common forms prolong the endless chain
> Of joy and grief, of pleasure and of pain.[2]

The earliest surviving version of *Guilt and Sorrow*, a long narrative poem in Spenserian stanzas, also dates from 1794. Wordsworth is again deeply engrossed in the problem of sympathy; but however subtle his inward workings, he has made no headway in expression. Indeed, since *Guilt and Sorrow* lacks the varnished anonymity of his meditative heroics, there is more violent absurdity in the sight of man and nature walking hand in hand through the poem, in overt congruity of mood.

> "O come," he cried, "come, after weary night
> So ominous, far other scene to view."
> So forth she came, and eastward looked; the sight
> Over her brow like dawn of gladness threw,
> That tinged with faint red smile her faded hue:
> Not lovelier did the morning star appear,
> Parting the lucid mist and bathed in dew:
> The whilst her comrade to her pensive cheer
> Tempered sweet words of hope; and the lark warbled near.[3]

Wordsworth said of *Guilt and Sorrow* that it was "addressed to coarse sympathies".[4] This is also true of *The Borderers*, which immediately succeeds it; but here, as in the history of the Wordsworthian solitaries, there are intimations of mature power. The pivot of the play,

---

[1] *P.W.*, Vol. I. p. 10.   [2] *Ibid.*, p. 13.
[3] *Ibid.*, p. 112.   [4] *Ibid.*, p. 334.

half obscured by the to and fro of Godwinian philosophizing, is a single star. Under the influence of
Oswald's sophistry, Marmaduke is on the point of
murdering Herbert, when he happens to raise his eyes:

> Upwards I cast my eyes, and, through a crevice,
> Beheld a star twinkling above my head,
> And, by the living God, I could not do it.[1]

Later in the play, when he is once more of Oswald's
persuasion, Marmaduke reflects upon this moment:

> Last night, when moved to lift the avenging steel,
> I did believe all things were shadows—yea,
> Living or dead all things were bodiless,
> Or but the mutual mockeries of body,
> Till that same star summoned me back again.
> Now I could laugh till my ribs ached. Oh, Fool!
> To let a creed, built in the heart of things,
> Dissolve before a twinkling atom![2]

A star prevents a murder: this is the point towards
which Wordsworth's prosings about the life of intellect
and the life of sensation are vainly directed. Hitherto,
sympathy has been simply a matter of external correspondence with environment. Wordsworth now tries to
say something more difficult. Oswald, we have seen,
stands for the isolation of intellect; and this isolation is
false because it is achieved only through the denial of
relationship. Wordsworth argues in his Preface that
Oswald's world is determined by his intellectualism: he
looks at things "through an optical glass of a peculiar
tint": the colour of objects "is exclusively what he
gives them; it is one, and it is his own". Since he can
only see things in this intellectual monochrome,
Oswald cannot see anything except himself. But
Marmaduke saw a star, and in so doing he realized
that Oswald's "creed" and the "twinkling atom" were

[1] l. 988. The early version is given in *P.W.*, Vol. I., p. 167.   [2] l. 1213.

at war. Wordsworth spends the next ten years showing what it means to see things: in *The Borderers* he makes a tentative beginning by contrasting Oswald's need, in false isolation, to

> turn perforce and seek for sympathy
> In dim relation to imagined Beings[1]

with Marmaduke's sudden wisdom in the presence of the star. This wisdom is the child of true sympathy, and true sympathy's other name is reciprocity, active relationship, or

> enobling interchange
> Of action from within and from without.[2]

Oswald's abstract creed made a ghost of the external world, "till that same star summoned me back again". *The Borderers* fails to impress the intervention of the star: it is merely suggested that the star showed Marmaduke that he had been wrong in supposing "all things were shadows". This association of the effectiveness of the world with its solidity is very characteristic of Wordsworth: he says of his Cumberland childhood:

> brought up in such a grand
> And lovely region, I had forms distinct
> To steady me . . . I still
> At all times had a real solid world
> Of images about me. . . .[3]

But of course this will not do by itself, and in *The Borderers* it goes unsupported.

The first book of *The Excursion* was conceived as an independent narrative poem. This poem, *The Ruined Cottage* or *The Pedlar*, was finished in the spring of

[1] l. 1454.   [2] *The Prelude*, Bk. XII. 376.
[3] *Ibid.*, Bk. VIII. 596.

1798, although there had once been a shorter version which Wordsworth read to Coleridge in the previous summer. As late as 1802, Wordsworth regarded *The Pedlar* as complete in itself, and was considering its publication. In date of composition it is close to *The Borderers*, but in little else; for *The Pedlar* takes a decisive step into maturity. Most of it is incorporated, with little change, in *The Excursion*, which shows that Wordsworth was prepared to stand by this early work in 1814, when he published *The Excursion*. The whole poem is charged with anticipation. Here, for example, is a foretaste of the 1800 Preface to the *Lyrical Ballads:*

> He from his native hills
> Had wandered far, much had he seen of men
> Their manners, their enjoyments and pursuits
> Their passions and their feelings, chiefly those
> Essential and eternal in the heart
> Which mid the simpler forms of rural life
> Exist more simple in their elements
> And speak a plainer language.[1]

This passage is taken from a long account of the Pedlar's early history which is itself autobiographical in spirit, and looks forward to *The Prelude*, where, in the 1805 text, much of it reappears unaltered.

The original *Pedlar* is thus a source poem of great importance. Furthermore, it has a personal merit easy to overlook in purely textual study. The first point of interest is its connexion with *The Old Cumberland Beggar*, written a few months before Wordsworth finished *The Pedlar*. In both these poems the relational power of the solitaries has a definite social aspect; but their roles are exactly opposed. The beggar binds the society through which he moves as recipient of elementary charities, his maintenance being accepted as a common duty; whereas the pedlar carries round with

[1] *P.W.*, Vol. V. p. 380. Compare *The Excursion*, Bk. I. 340.

him the means of satisfying the needs of a scattered, simple-living community, "all dependant", Wordsworth says, "upon the Pedlar's toil". And each of these cyclical wanderers is brought to his own "vast solitude".

The poem opens with Wordsworth's chance arrival at a ruined and deserted cottage where he meets an old pedlar, already well known to him. There follows a description of the pedlar's early childhood, which opens, feebly enough, with a few lines of gothic stage-setting:

> I loved to hear him talk of former days
> And tell how when a child, ere yet of age
> To be a shepherd, he had learned to read
> His bible in a school that stood alone,
> Sole building on a mountain's dreary edge,
> Far from the sight of city spire, or sound
> Of Minster clock.[1]

But the account of the child's education, with which Wordsworth continues, is of different quality. As in *The Prelude*, Wordsworth talks about the influence of nature and of books: in particular, he is attentive to the way in which the child relates his earliest understanding of mathematics to the natural objects around him:

> While yet he linger'd in the elements
> Of science, and among her simplest laws,
> His triangles, they were the stars of heaven,
> The *silent* stars; his altitudes the crag
> Which is the eagle's birthplace; or some peak
> Familiar with forgotten years, which shews,
> Inscribed, as with the silence of the thought,
> Upon its bleak and visionary sides,
> The history of many a winter storm,
> Or obscure records of the path of fire.[2]

[1] *P.W.*, Vol. V. p. 380.
[2] *Ibid.*, p. 384. Compare *The Excursion*, Bk. I. 270.

There is no passage in Wordsworth more important than this, for it makes the main argument of his poetry brilliantly clear. The juvenile and clumsy statements of sympathy, in terms of open correspondence between inner and outer, are in fact directed towards the experience which Wordsworth here describes. The child does not learn about one world of unchanging abstract types, of mental stuff, and about a second, shifting world of natural objects. He learns about a single world in which triangles march about the sky, in which mountain-sides are suffering things, and also quietly, mathematically, eternal. The mountain with a history of violence "inscribed as with the silence of the thought" upon its sides is profoundly Words-worthian in its command of mental and physical. And so my account of relationship, as of solitude, becomes a tale of dualisms ultimately daunting to intellect but mastered in poetry. Wordsworth remembered how the child had seen things when he came to write about the Danish Boy singing at once of love and war, Lucy in silent sympathy with wind and stars and perfectly alone, the discharged soldier, like the mountain, a living history, the old man walking with thought and towards peace, yet walking; the Leech-Gatherer, entirely eloquent.

The Pedlar deals thus with the visionary power of childhood:

> Ere his ninth summer he was sent abroad
> To tend his father's sheep, such was his task
> Henceforward to the later day of youth.
> Oh! then what soul was his when on the tops
> Of the high mountains he beheld the sun
> Rise up and bathe the world in light. He looked,
> The ocean and the earth beneath him lay
> In gladness and deep joy. The clouds were touched
> And in their silent faces did he read

Unutterable love. Sound needed none
Nor any voice of joy: his spirit drank
The spectacle. Sensation, soul and form
All melted into him. They swallowed up
His animal being; in them did he live
And by them did he live. They were his life.[1]

There are many passages, in *The Prelude* especially,
very close to this in their manner of proceeding; nor is
this by any means as good as the best, so that there is
less to lose in using it roughly, to point a general moral.
The opening is level-toned, the impression of quiet
narrative conveyed by preliminary mention of age and
occupation, and sustained by adherence to prose-order
for nearly ten lines. In its ease and length of stride,
Wordsworth's language wears its blank verse form
very lightly. The vocabulary is characteristically
limited, but of an elemental strength, building on the
Wordsworthian bed-rock of earth, ocean, sun, cloud
and mountain. As always, the spareness of texture that
is not quite meanness is enforced by a profusion of
monosyllables—two of the first six lines are entirely
monosyllabic. Adjectives are few and carefully chosen:
"high" and "deep" bind mathematical quantity to
nature qualitative and sentient; and the faces of the
clouds are "silent". "Unutterable", a sudden poly-
syllabic blaze, marks a decisive shift of mood. The
change is at once apparent. In "sound needed none"
there is both poetic omission and inversion. The periods
become suddenly short and choppy, dragooned into
blank verse. The vocabulary reaches out towards
science and philosophy.

This is not altogether a success. The careful development towards "unutterable love" is marred by "Oh!
then what soul was his. . . ."—an invitation to ecstasy
delivered too soon and too crudely. But the real crux

[1] *P.W.*, Vol. V. p. 382. Compare *The Excursion*, Bk. I. 197.

rests in the second part of the passage, where Wordsworth addresses himself to the child's experience in two
different ways. On the one hand, he resorts to huge,
opaque technicalities—"sensation", "soul", "form"
—worn smooth in centuries of speculative use. On the
other, he describes the child's relation with his world
by means of a single metaphor. He "drank" the scene,
and the scene "swallowed" him; so that Wordsworth
concludes, emerging from the violent particularity of
this image, that the scene lived in him and he in it.
Here two methods of approach consort a little un-
easily, and in consequence they both attract the wrong
sort of attention. "Sensation, soul and form" looks like
an intellectual smoke-screen, hastily laid to conceal a
false move in argument: we ask what it means, and find
it contorted and pretentiously obscure. This leaves the
metaphor exposed in a way it can ill afford. Isolated, it is
a blunt and conventional device; and, in its reciprocal
reference to child and scene, somewhat grotesque.

Even if unsuccessful, this passage from *The Pedlar*
is very instructive. Elsewhere Wordsworth uses a
vocabulary strong in intellectual associations: it is this
that has led critics to impose a formal philosophical
interpretation upon *The Prelude* which I do not think
it will bear. My discussion of solitude and relationship
is not intended to deny that Wordsworth was in some
sense influenced by Locke and Hartley; or even to
prefer Spinoza before them; but rather to show that
when he writes good poetry his language of intellect is
successfully directed to a further end. In *The Pedlar*
this language seems misty and unattached because
Wordsworth fails to refer it to the purpose sleeping in
his rough and very concrete metaphor. For a bald
summary of this purpose we must return to Wordsworth's statement of aims in the Prospectus to *The
Recluse*.[1] He hopes to reveal the exquisite fitting of

[1] See p. 41.

the mind and the external world, each to the other, and

> the creation (by no lower name
> Can it be called) which they with blended might
> Accomplish:—this is our high argument.[1]

This feeding on one another of the child and the visible scene is a typical statement of the fact of mutual fitting. The relationship is stable, both terms being wholly taken up in interaction whereby, through supporting each other they support themselves. Wordsworth develops this "interchange of action from within and from without" in a number of ways. The metaphor used in *The Pedlar* is a favourite. So is the silent dialogue in which each perfectly understands the other; and, close to this, the partnership in music-making—the Eolian Harp image in the first book of *The Prelude* is particularly fine.[2] Again, he talks of the mind as "wedded to this goodly universe",[3] and *The Prelude* is rich in images of communion and intercourse, though of sacramental rather than sexual quality. This concert of imagery lays stress on the difference between Wordsworth and Coleridge laboured in my first chapter. Both were natural monists, but the theme of the one was unity and of the other significant relation. Success meant for Coleridge the building of his dome in air, and failure the involuntary egotism of *The Dejection Ode:*

> O Lady! we receive but what we give,
> And in our life alone does Nature live.

Wordsworth could not have written this, as is evident even in his attempts to convey the whole truth in a phrase, in the largest of his reality-metaphors where he is driven as it were to reify relationship, so that in a general though unhelpful way one may talk about unity with reference to him as to anybody professing to make

[1] l. 69.   [2] ll. 101-7.   [3] Preface to *The Excursion*, l. 53.

sense of things. Reality in *The Prelude* is a building, a
frame or a fabric—a complex of mutually sustaining
elements. The word "unity", in all its forms, appears
only twice in the entire poem,[1] and on the first of these
occasions with direct reference to Coleridge, as one to
whom "the unity of all has been revealed". On the
other hand Wordsworth falls back three times in the
first three books upon the various forms of "link"[2] in
order to express his relational principle; and even the
outlandish "collateral", with its adverb, is pressed
twice in the first two books into the same service.[3] Only
a fool would be guided by vocabulary alone, but it
remains noteworthy that Wordsworth's concentration
of effort is reflected at every level of seriousness.

Of Wordsworth's reality-metaphors, that of landscape is by far the most commanding. But since his
landscapes do not reflect or represent or point towards
absent realities, it were less confusing to talk about
landscape than about metaphor, or about reality. There
is an inclusive literalness about these landscapes to
which we are introduced by *The Pedlar*. The child's
stars are his triangles, and his mountain-peaks his alti-
tudes—a blunt assertion at once justified in the
strength of "inscribed as with the silence of the
thought". Shelley spoke of Wordsworth as "wakening
a sort of thought in sense"[4]; and he should be heeded.
In the first book of *The Prelude* Wordsworth refers,
with reference to earliest childhood, to

> Those hallow'd and pure motions of the sense
> Which seem in their simplicity to own
> An intellectual charm, that calm delight
> Which, if I err not, surely must belong

[1] Bk. II. 226; Bk. VIII. 826.
[2] Bk. I. 601; Bk. I. 639; Bk. III. 127.
[3] Bk. I. 621; Bk. II. 52.
[4] *Peter Bell the Third*.

> To those first-born affinities that fit
> Our new existence to existing things,
> And, in our dawn of being, constitute
> The bond of union betwixt life and joy.[1]

And, later on, he speaks of

> The gravitation and the filial bond
> Of nature, that connect him with the world.[2]

The child is "an inmate of this *active* universe" where he "creates, creator and receiver both":

> Such, verily, is the first
> Poetic spirit of our human life;
> By uniform control of after years
> In most abated or suppress'd, in some,
> Through every change of growth or of decay,
> Pre-eminent till death.

The child is wholly and unselfconsciously involved in this universal life of action and reaction. But the poet's participation cannot be in this manner complete, because he must reflect upon and express the condition of thought-in-sense which the child merely experiences. Hence the problem of poetry is for Wordsworth primarily one of self-awareness. The poet must experience thought-in-sense if he is to have anything to say, but if he is ever to say it, he must be aware of his experience. Experience without reflection means an inarticulate living of poetry—an idea near to Wordsworth's heart—and reflection on experience once past, poetic suicide. Thus the whole weight of Wordsworth's theory of poetry rests upon the poetic memory, in which the adult can return to his experience without bringing back with him, in any destructive way, the distinction between thought and sense which he has necessarily come to live by. And so "the first poetic spirit" is in some "pre-eminent till death".

[1] l. 578.   [2] Bk. II. 263.

Wordsworth's poetic memory is a sustained paradox. The poet loses himself and finds himself; he recovers the childish condition, yet he knows what he is doing when in poetry he wakens thought-in-sense. Once again, a general comparison with Spinoza is illuminating. Rather as the philosopher argues for an all-embracing Substance in which his reasoning self must somehow be contained, the poet is both experiencing, or re-experiencing, thought-in-sense, and telling the tale, at once inside and outside his "active universe".

This operation of memory, which Wordsworth more than once fails to expound in prose, is demonstrated in his poetry. *The Pedlar* makes a beginning, though still too expository for entire success: it is marred by an intellectual perseverance, sometimes shrill and heckling in tone, for the most part heavily didactic, which is the vice of Wordsworth's longer poems. The child instinctively held together abstract knowledge and natural appearance in one society.

> with her [Nature's] hues,
> Her forms, and with the spirit of her forms,
> He clothed the nakedness of austere truth.[1]

But as he grew up this "just equipoise" became harder to maintain: the state of thought-in-sense was giving place to a fearful tension:

> But now, before his twentieth year was pass'd,
> Accumulated feelings press'd his heart
> With an encreasing weight; he was o'er power'd
> By Nature, and his mind became disturbed,
> And many a time he wished the winds might rage
> When they were silent: from his intellect,
> And from the stillness of abstracted thought,
> In vain he sought repose, in vain he turned
> To science for a cure.

---

[1] *P.W.*, Vol. V. p. 384.

G

Even so, there could be no complete denial of his past; for he retained the memory of what he had been, and sometimes, in moments of insight, he returned to his early peace:

> From Nature and her overflowing soul
> He had received so much, that all his thoughts
> Were steeped in feeling. He was only then
> Contented, when, with bliss ineffable
> He felt the sentiment of being, spread
> O'er all that moves, and all that seemeth still,
> O'er all which, lost beyond the reach of thought,
> And human knowledge, to the human eye
> Invisible, yet liveth to the heart,
> O'er all that leaps, and runs, and shouts, and sings,
> Or beats the gladsome air, o'er all that glides
> Beneath the wave, yea in the wave itself
> And mighty depth of waters. Wonder not
> If such his transports were; for in all things
> He saw one life, and felt that it was joy.
> One song they sang, and it was audible,
> Most audible then, when the fleshly ear
> O'ercome by grosser prelude of that strain,
> Forgot its functions, and slept undisturbed.

This passage, which appears almost unaltered in the 1805 *Prelude*,[1] is bent towards the poetic state of recovered integration. The "sentiment of being, spread over all"; the universal sympathetic movement; the "one life" and the "one song"—all reflect Wordsworthian permanence in process and the condition of entire and urgent involvement:

> All things shall live in us and we shall live
> In all things that surround us.[2]

Wisely, Wordsworth avoids any exposition of the working of thought and sense at the moment of insight:

[1] Bk. II. 416.   [2] *P.W.*, Vol. V. p. 402.

the poetic understanding touched things "lost beyond
the reach of thought", and the poetic hearing was
keenest when "the fleshly ear . . . forgot its functions,
and slept undisturbed". Paradox had better be called
paradox, though not too loudly. Later in *The Pedlar*
Wordsworth returns to the problem, and achieves only
a false explicitness:

> thus the senses and the intellect
> Shall each to each supply a mutual aid,
> Invigorate and sharpen and refine
> Each other with a power that knows no bound. . . .[1]

This sort of thing invites a specifically intellectual
criticism that it cannot withstand.

Wordsworth describes the condition of insight as a
kind of alert day-dream, an inclusive state, like that of
the Leech-Gatherer, embracing waking life, and sleep,
and death. Thus the famous account, in *Tintern Abbey*, of

> that blessed mood,
> In which the burthen of the mystery,
> In which the heavy and the weary weight
> Of all this unintelligible world,
> Is lightened:—that serene and blessed mood,
> In which the affections gently lead us on,—
> Until, the breath of this corporeal frame
> And even the motion of our human blood
> Almost suspended, we are laid asleep
> In body, and become a living soul:
> While with an eye made quiet by the power
> Of harmony, and the deep power of joy,
> We see into the life of things.

The "eye made quiet" is the key that opens all doors,
the supreme poetic agent considered by nineteenth-
century criticism in such terms as "meditative pathos"
—with more sense of direction, I have tried to show,

1 *P.W.*, Vol. V. p. 402.

than subsequent embroiderers of the theme of Wordsworth's mystical sense of unity with nature. The eye
made quiet is the relational principle in action, "looking
for the shades of difference As they lie hid in all
exterior forms", and at the same time observing
"affinities In objects where no brotherhood exists To
common minds".[1] In *Tintern Abbey* it is referred to the
beautiful and the intelligible: not frenziedly—no
"dying in a dance", no Keatsian rich urgency; but
with gentle insistence to record, in the *Prelude* phrase,
"a register of permanent relations".[2] The eye made
quiet is thought-in-sense reborn.

At the end of *The Pedlar* Wordsworth attempts to
state the terms of a private discipline through which the
regeneration of thought-in-sense may be achieved; and
again, in his *Letter to Mathetes*, published by Coleridge
in his journal, *The Friend*. What advice, Wordsworth
asks, can be offered to one who has recently lost his
childhood?

> He cannot recall past time; he cannot begin his journey
> afresh; he cannot untwist the links by which, in no undelight-
> ful harmony, images and sentiments are wedded in his mind.
> Granted that the sacred light of childhood is and must be for
> him no more than a remembrance. He may, notwithstanding,
> be remanded to Nature; and with trustworthy hopes; founded
> less upon his sentient than upon his intellectual being—to
> Nature, not as leading on insensibly to the society of Reason;
> but to Reason and Will, as leading back to the wisdom of
> Nature. A reunion, in this order accomplished, will bring
> reformation and timely support; and the two powers of
> Reason and Nature, thus reciprocally teacher and taught,
> may advance together in a track to which there is no limit.

This is a distinct echo of the mutual support of senses
and intellect for which Wordsworth argues in *The
Pedlar*. But there is an air of futility about discursive

---

[1] *The Prelude*, Bk. III. 158; Bk. II. 403.   [2] Bk. II. 311.

accounts of this kind: they lack the force of Wordsworth's open appeal to the poetic memory in his
deriving of poetry from emotion recollected in tranquillity, and in his *Prelude* distinction between remembering *how* and remembering *what*[1] upon which he rests
the "sense of possible sublimity".

While analysis of thought-in-sense is in the nature of
the thing a hopeless venture, Wordsworth has left an
interesting note of its psychology. Referring to the
Prelude passage about the boy who hooted to the owls,
which he published as a separate poem, he says:

> The Boy, there introduced, is listening with something of
> a feverish and restless anxiety for the recurrence of those
> riotous sounds which he had previously excited; and at the
> moment when the intenseness of his mind is beginning to
> remit, he is surprised into a perception of the solemn and
> tranquillizing images which the Poem describes.[2]

Now here are the relevant lines of the poem:

> And, when there came a pause
> Of silence such as baffled his best skill:
> Then, sometimes, in that silence, while he hung
> Listening, a gentle shock of mild surprise
> Has carried far into his heart the voice
> Of mountain-torrents; or the visible scene
> Would enter unawares into his mind
> With all its solemn imagery, its rocks,
> Its woods, and that uncertain heaven received
> Into the bosom of the steady lake.[3]

[1] See p. 70.

[2] Preface to the 1815 Edition of Wordsworth's Poems.

[3] *The Prelude*, Bk. V. 404. That the account is autobiographical is shown
by the fact that Wordsworth's earliest draft is written in the first person (de
Selincourt, p. 608 D). De Quincey has a story about Wordsworth that
exactly corresponds to Wordsworth's own note to *There Was a Boy*. De
Quincey's story is quoted, in different connexions, by Professor Beatty
(*William Wordsworth*, p. 160), N. P. Stallknecht (*Strange Seas of Thought*,
p. 60), and Dr Helen Darbishire (*The Poet Wordsworth*, p. 110).

The attention is entirely focused upon one object: then, as relaxation sets in, there is a moment of vulnerability. The child, or the poet, has trained all his conscious powers in one direction, and "he is surprised into a perception" before he can recover his normal balance. He is caught in mid-stride, as concentration fades, between one daylight condition and the next.

Wordsworth says, in *Tintern Abbey*, that once we have gained an eye made quiet, we "see into the life of things". The life of things he thought of primarily and to best effect as landscape. *There was a Boy* is in point: there thought-in-sense is presented as a state of exposure in which, because it has ceased to maintain the ordinary waking distinction between inner and outer, the mind is penetrated by the visible scene. This penetration, insisted on in "carried far into his heart" and "would enter unawares into his mind", is the very nerve of Wordsworth's literal genius; and the tendency to pass it by as weakly metaphorical results from inattention to his received modes of thought as to the nature of selfconsciousness. In the rationalist tradition, knowledge of the self is different in kind and superior in certainty to knowledge of the external world acquired through the senses; but an eighteenth-century empiricist regarded self-knowledge as the fruit of introspection, a sixth and inner sense, comparable in its working to the five external senses. Nor was this simply a matter between philosophers: it had, and still has, a profound effect on the assumptions of unreflective people. What distinguishes Wordsworth is the enormous importance which he attaches to introspection, or the inward eye. He believed in it with a seriousness attainable only by men of power.

The first consequence of Wordsworth's belief in the inward eye is a granting of extension to the inward world which it surveys. De Quincey makes a relevant comment on the poem which we have just been considering:

> The very expression "far" by which space and its infinities are attributed to the human heart, and its capacities of re-echoing the sublimities of nature, has always struck me as with a flash of sublime revelation.[1]

Wordsworth is as much in earnest about the inward world's extension as he is about the outward world's capacity to suffer. Here, where he emphasizes the heart's depth, his theme is penetration: in *Tintern Abbey* he speaks of sensations "felt along the heart", and the inward world is a wide coastline; for in that poem, as we shall see, the two face each other like sea and land.

In his dealings with the inward as with the outward world, Wordsworth depends upon landscape: he is constantly referring to the landscape of the mind, and he approaches his perennial problem of sympathy as one of apparent opposition between the two landscapes. *Tintern Abbey* is distinguished by its opening words from *There was a Boy* and from an even more famous poem about his earlier life: "There was a time when meadow, grove, and stream. . . ." Both of these are thrown—this use of the verb "to be" is quite characteristic—into a remote story-teller's past, larger than human, invested with the authority of myth; whereas *Tintern Abbey*, being concerned to relate two distinct points in time, begins: "Five years have past. . . ."

The occasion of *Tintern Abbey* is Wordsworth's return to a particular countryside, after an absence of five years. He thinks it important that the scene is outwardly unchanged, and that he stands in the very place where he then stood: "again" is reiterated four times in the first fifteen lines, and his own position pinpointed by "here, under this dark sycamore". Words-

---

[1] De Quincey, *Literary Reminiscences* (Boston, 1874). See p. 91 n.

worth's return leads him to reflect on the landscape
seen five years ago, on the landscape before him today,
and on the landscape which he has carried about with
him during his absence. The brutal contrast between
then and now is for a moment disquieting:

> And now, with gleams of half-extinguished thought,
> And many recognitions dim and faint,
> And somewhat of a sad perplexity,
> The picture of the mind revives again:
> While here I stand. . . .

But this is a fleeting shadow across a poem of steady
and shining optimism. As he stands before the familiar
scene, Wordsworth is convinced "that in this moment
there is life and food For future years" because this
same scene has proved its strength while he has been
away from it. In *The Pedlar* Wordsworth asks whether
it can have been meant that the natural world,

> the clouds,
> The ocean, and the firmament of heaven
> Should lie a barren picture on the mind ?[1]

and he argues that when we have entered into a truly
reciprocal relationship, into

> quiet sympathies with things that hold
> An inarticulate language,

we

> shall discover what a power is theirs
> To stimulate our minds, and multiply
> The spiritual presences of absent things.[2]

Tintern Abbey is addressed to the fact of spiritual
presence enduring through physical absence. The
opposition of the landscape before him at this passing
moment and the landscape before him at another

---

[1] *P.W.*, Vol. V. p. 402.   [2] *Ibid.*, p. 400.

moment five years ago, "the picture of the mind" now suddenly recalled, is not final; for Wordsworth has knowledge of a third landscape.

> These beauteous forms,
> Through a long absence, have not been to me
> As is a landscape to a blind man's eye. . . .

And he proceeds to declare his indebtedness to absent things. His chief debt to this third landscape, a gift, he calls it, "of aspect more sublime", is the eye made quiet, which comprehends both the inward and the outward eye. By means of it he can gaze upon, and yet maintain his place and active function within, the larger landscape of Wordsworthian reality.

The Immortality Ode also has important things to say about the third landscape. The child lives naturally and wholeheartedly within it, for as yet he knows nothing of the other two. This Wordsworth has already explained, and at much greater length, in *The Pedlar* and *The Prelude*. Wordsworth's comment on the Ode[1] speaks of his own "absolute spirituality" and "all-soulness" in childhood; and its first two stanzas open with cascading images of splendour in which this condition is evoked as an inclusive natural grace—"innocent brightness" in the last stanza is a key—both ethical and aesthetic in quality; the stanzas ending, in each case, with an antiphonal lament for departed vision.

In the third stanza Wordsworth moves from the loss of childish integrity to its sudden recovery in poetic expression:

> Now, while the birds thus sing a joyous song,
> And while the young lambs bound
> As to the tabor's sound,
> To me alone there came a thought of grief:
> A timely utterance gave that thought relief,
> And I again am strong. . . .

[1] Grosart, Vol. III. p. 464.

He then states the meaning of this regained strength:

> The cataracts blow their trumpets from the steep;
> No more shall grief of mine the season wrong;
> I hear the Echoes through the mountains throng,
> The Winds come to me from the fields of sleep. . . .

And later in the Ode he has a few lines on the same subject:

> Hence in a season of calm weather
> Though inland far we be,
> Our souls have sight of that immortal sea
> Which brought us hither,
> Can in a moment travel thither,
> And see the Children sport upon the shore. . . .

About this treatment of recovered powers there is a supreme concentration and a finality: it bears a weight of poetic thought sustained through many years, and it regards Wordsworth's greater landscape with the steadiness and penetration of a dying gaze. Everything is here. The season of calm weather is the eye made quiet, the means of insight. The fields of sleep, not quite Elysian nor yet St Augustine's Fields of Memory, the home of insight, where, as again in "though inland far we be", the poet walks through time as he walks through space. The features of this greater landscape are wind, water, mountain, and echo. These bind the Ode to the poetry that precedes it.

Celebrating his escape from city life in the opening lines of *The Prelude*, Wordsworth turns first of all towards the wind.

> Oh there is blessing in this gentle breeze
> That blows from the green fields and from the clouds
> And from the sky: it beats against my cheek
> And seems half-conscious of the joy it gives.

For the wind brings with it the promise of life lived
with understanding:

> I breathe again;
> Trances of thought and mountings of the mind
> Come fast upon me. . . .

And it arouses a counterpart to itself within the poet:

> For I, methought, while the sweet breath of heaven
> Was blowing on my body, felt within
> A corresponding mild creative breeze,
> A vital breeze which travell'd gently on
> O'er things which it had made, and is become
> A tempest, a redundant energy
> Vexing its own creation.

Then, after recounting how for a time he gave "a
respite to this passion", Wordsworth again calls upon
the wind:

> It was a splendid evening; and my soul
> Did once again make trial of the strength
> Restored to her afresh; nor did she want
> Eolian visitations; but the harp
> Was soon defrauded, and the banded host
> Of harmony dispers'd in straggling sounds
> And, lastly, utter silence.

The wind that searches the *Prelude* landscape is from
the beginning of the world, aboriginal in its command
of the ideas, long since estranged, of breath, of vital
spirit, and of inspiration. In this wind's ebb and flow
Wordsworth demonstrates the fitting of mind and
external things, as in the Eolian harp image, or when
he finds himself in the face of nature

> obedient as a lute
> That waits upon the touches of the wind.[1]

1 Bk. III. 137.

Thus he can speak at once of a partnership in harmony and of a single song resulting. As it passes freely between inward and outward, familiar with both and native to neither, the wind manifests universal coherence; so that with every breath we draw, according to the poet's childlike metaphysic, we say "Boo" to a philosophical goose over-anxious about the difference between himself and other things.

The wind is also important to Wordsworth because it comprehends vitality and movement, ideas finally inseparable to his understanding. In two passages, both written in Germany, he saw the world a cold star, wheeling through Galilean skies. Lucy, motionless in death, was

> Roll'd round in earth's diurnal course,
> With rocks, and stones, and trees.

And the skating adventures of *The Prelude* led him to a strangely severe vision:

> then at once
> Have I, reclining back upon my heels,
> Stopp'd short, yet still the solitary cliffs
> Wheeled by me, even as if the earth had roll'd
> With visible motion her diurnal round. . . .[1]

But much more characteristic of Wordsworth is a movement instinct with breath, as when he

> felt the sentiment of Being spread
> O'er all that moves and all that seemeth still.[2]

Or, in *Tintern Abbey* lines that compare with the German passages in vastness of conception and in which the cosmic "roll" appears for a third time, when he encountered

> A motion and a spirit, that impels
> All thinking things, all objects of all thought,
> And rolls through all things.

[1] Bk. I. 482. [2] Bk. II. 420.

In *The Prelude* Wordsworth apostrophizes the
"Wisdom and Spirit of the universe" as giving "to
forms and images a breath And everlasting motion":
but his frequent habit of entrusting movement to breath
itself, without any personification, is much more effective. "All that I beheld," he says, "respired with inward meaning"; and the ceaseless to and fro of this
universal breath is meaningful in its power to comprehend the moving and the vital. He speaks of "breathing
sea", "breathing air", "breathing frame", and, many
times, of "breathing world", to convey a surging life
or a living surge, eternal and intelligible.

Breath is also closely associated with urgent spiritual
presence. Thus he describes the thought of an absent
person as being like "an *unseen* companionship, a
breath"; and when in his childhood he stole game from
another boy's snare, he says he

> heard among the solitary hills
> Low breathings coming after me, and sounds
> Of undistinguishable motion, steps
> Almost as silent as the turf they trod.[1]

Allied to this is the peculiar animation which he im-
parts to abstract nouns, among other means by coupling
them with breath: things and persons in his poetry
breath "life", "sweetness", "invitation", "tenderness", "intelligence", "immortality".

In *Michael*, written in 1800, the wind becomes the
focus of an entire poetic attitude: the optimistic naturalism of the Great Decade stands or falls by it. Michael
is a relational solitary in the classical tradition; a shepherd, a very old man who has reached perfect solitude
through perfect sympathy with his environment. When
Wordsworth introduces him he makes his understanding of the wind the measure of this perfection:

[1] *The Prelude*, Bk. I. 329.

> in his shepherd's calling he was prompt
> And watchful more than ordinary men.
> Hence had he learnt the meaning of all winds,
> And blasts of every tone; and oftentimes,
> When others heeded not, He heard the South
> Make subterraneous music, like the noise
> Of bagpipers on distant Highland hills.
> The Shepherd, at such warning, of his flock
> Bethought him, and he to himself would say,
> "The winds are now devising work for me!"
> And, truly, at all times, the storm, that drives
> The traveller to a shelter, summoned him
> Up to the mountains: he had been alone
> Amid the heart of many thousand mists,
> That came to him, and left him, on the heights.

Michael has a son whom he brings up to succeed him as a shepherd. But suddenly, and through no fault of his own, he loses much of his money, and decides to send Luke, the son, to seek his fortune in the town so that the land, the family inheritance, may be saved.

> Our Luke shall leave us, Isabel; the land
> Shall not go from us, and it shall be free;
> He shall possess it, free as is the wind
> That passes over it.

For a time all goes well, and Luke sends home "loving letters, full of wondrous news". Then disaster follows, reported in an external, uncomprehending way that makes Luke's new environment infinitely remote from the one already described. This is typical of Wordsworth's use of the city as a pasteboard symbol of vice and artifice, the home of the unintelligible, the wholly random element in things:

> Meantime Luke began
> To slacken in his duty; and, at length,
> He in the dissolute city gave himself

> To evil courses: ignominy and shame
> Fell on him, so that he was driven at last
> To seek a hiding-place beyond the seas.

And the poem at once returns to Michael and his shepherding, its cyclical movement supported by the exact repetition of several of its opening phrases, and by "still" and "as before"; so that it ends as it began, considering sun and cloud and eloquent wind—"in truth", Wordsworth says, "an utter solitude".

> Among the rocks
> He went, and still looked up to sun and cloud,
> And listened to the wind; and, as before,
> Performed all kinds of labour for his sheep,
> And for the land, his small inheritance.

Although it lacks the clear design of *Michael*, *The Prelude* also looks to the wind for a vindication of its world. In the childhood adventures there is a strong metaphysical undertow to the wind's working, as in the way it supported and at the same time admonished Wordsworth while he hung

> Above the raven's nest, by knots of grass
> And half-inch fissures in the slippery rock
> But ill-sustain'd, and almost, as it seem'd,
> Suspended by the blast that blew amain,
> Shouldering the naked crag; Oh! at that time,
> While on the perilous ridge I hung alone,
> With what strange utterance did the loud dry wind
> Blow through my ears![1]

As in *Michael*, the wind is the idea of a world bound together in discourse with itself. "I would stand," he says, again of his childhood,

> Beneath some rock, listening to sounds that are
> The ghostly language of the ancient earth,
> Or make their dim abode in distant winds.
> Thence did I drink the visionary power.[2]

[1] Bk. I. 342.   [2] Bk. II. 327.

And this language is also spoken by the poet, for it is common to the entire universe of solitude in relationship, in which he lives "an equal among mighty energies". Wordsworth brings art and nature together in terms of a shared speech. He who "with living Nature hath been intimate" receives knowledge and joy, "in measure only dealt out to himself", from

> the great Nature that exists in works
> Of mighty Poets. Visionary Power
> Attends upon the motions of the winds
> Embodied in the mystery of words.[1]

The wind, Wordsworth repeats, is the means of visionary power; of effective understanding reached through movement and life, and the mind's marriage "to this goodly universe In love and holy passion".

This single element within Wordsworth's greater landscape is managed with extreme subtlety. Consider, again from *The Prelude*, a horseback expedition to a ruined abbey,

> which within the Vale
> Of Nightshade, to St Mary's honour built,
> Stands yet, a mouldering pile, with fractured Arch,
> Belfry, and Images, and living Trees,
> A holy Scene! Along the smoooth green turf
> Our horses grazed: to more than inland peace
> Left by the sea wind passing overhead
> (Though wind of roughest temper) trees and towers
> May in that Valley oftentimes be seen,
> Both silent and both motionless alike;
> Such is the shelter that is there, and such
> The safeguard for repose and quietness.
>
> Our steeds remounted, and the summons given,
> With whip and spur we by the Chauntry flew
> In uncouth race, and left the cross-legg'd Knight,

[1] Bk. V. 618.

And the stone-Abbot, and that single Wren
Which one day sang so sweetly in the Nave
Of the old Church, that, though from recent showers
The earth was comfortless, and, touch'd by faint
Internal breezes, sobbings of the place,
And respirations, from the roofless walls
The shuddering ivy dripp'd large drops, yet still,
So sweetly 'mid the gloom the invisible Bird
Sang to itself, that there I could have made
My dwelling-place, and lived for ever there
To hear such music.[1]

Most of the vices of the 1805 *Prelude* are discovered in this passage. It is so loose in grammatical construction and so erratically punctuated[2] as to weary, almost to confuse, the reader: wordy, here and there shambling in its movement and in its diction disputably chaste. At the same time it has a personal logic that recalls Wordsworth's original intention, "to give pictures of Nature, Man, and Society". Like the more famous pictures of the *Prelude* Exhibition, it is a finished composition, hanging framed upon the wall.

Wordsworth is once more concerned with sympathy, as he comes upon it in the "more than inland peace" of the Nightshade valley. The valley is isolated, and the bounds of Wordsworth's picture determined, by the failure of the violent sea wind to break in upon it from the outside world; and in coupling the abbey towers with the living trees in their stillness and silence he indicates that the subject of his study is a building that has come in its old age to terms with its surroundings. There is a striking imaginative consistency in the way Wordsworth's lonely buildings (for this is one among many) are placed, like his human solitaries, at the extreme of life.

[1] Bk. II. 110.
[2] I have given "along" a capital letter where W. does not, in order to make the sense clearer.

Within this old church, "the cross-legg'd Knight, and the stone-Abbot, and that single Wren", thus huddled together in apparent carelessness, form a single society to which the boy is admitted for a moment. If in fact Wordsworth had "lived for ever there", the knight and the abbot would always have stayed with him, and the bird would not have ceased to sing. The strength of the passage is its association of art and nature. The stone figures are the church's proper inhabitants, Wordsworthian "Presences", graven and alive like mountains; and about the invisible wren there is the suggestion of eternal artifact, of the bird "set upon a golden bough to sing" in Yeats's Byzantium. While still a thing made with hands, the church that contains them all has made acquaintance with the natural: open to the sky, ivy-clad, stirred by internal breezes, sobbing, gently breathing—without facile identification or analogy Wordsworth has resolved it into his greater landscape.

Echo is understood, rather like wind and breath, as a relational and binding force. In one of his *Poems on the Naming of Places*, Wordsworth describes how, while he was walking with Joanna Hutchinson, his eye was held by the beauty of the scene before him, and she, noticing his eager gaze, "laughed aloud":

> The Rock, like something starting from a sleep,
> Took up the Lady's voice, and laughed again;
> That ancient Woman seated on Helm-crag
> Was ready with her cavern; Hammar-scar,
> And the tall Steep of Silver-how, sent forth
> A noise of laughter; southern Loughrigg heard,
> And Fairfield answered with a mountain tone;
> Helvellyn far into the clear blue sky
> Carried the Lady's voice,—old Skiddaw blew
> His speaking-trumpet;—back out of the clouds
> Of Glaramara southward came the voice;

And Kirkstone tossed it from his misty head.
—Now whether . . . this were in simple truth
A work accomplished by the brotherhood
Of ancient mountains, or my ear was touched
With dreams and visionary impulses
To me alone imparted, sure I am
That there was a loud uproar in the hills.[1]

Wordsworth's use of echo is quite simply effective as a roll-call, answered by the individual peaks when they are identified by name: thus the surrounding hills are enfolded into a single community, or "brotherhood"; for the work of echo is assisted by a characteristic family-metaphor.

Reflection, especially water-reflection, is very near to echo in the way it expounds Wordsworth's universe by collating different modes of being. Being is a key word: when Wordsworth sees "the sentiment of being spread over all", he is affirming the relational monism of his poetic faith and urging that the acknowledged diversity of things has its issue in a single complex, or "register of permanent relations". Reflection serves this end through balance and a very peculiar stability.

Thus having reached a bridge, that overarched
The hasty rivulet where it lay becalmed
In a deep pool, by happy chance we saw
A twofold image; on a grassy bank
A snow-white ram, and in the crystal flood
Another and the same! Most beautiful,
On the green turf, with his imperial front
Shaggy and bold, and wreathèd horns superb,
The breathing creature stood; as beautiful,
Beneath him, showed his shadowy counterpart.
Each had his glowing mountains, each his sky,
And each seemed centre of his own fair world:

[1] *To Joanna.*

Antipodes unconscious of each other,
Yet, in partition, with their several spheres,
Blended in perfect stillness, to our sight![1]

This is no ordinary reflection: the independence of the ram beneath the water is so insisted on throughout the passage that one cannot regard it as deriving its existence from the ram upon the bank. It is a distinct mode of being, self-sufficient in its nether world. Yet the two rams are not unconnected, for they are finally contained within a single picture, their connexion in distinctness beautifully foreshown in the antipodean image. Peculiar to Wordsworth is the way this single vision is achieved without sacrificing either of the rams. He does not reduce the second to a mere emanation from the living reality, nor the first to a gross and earthly instance of the ideal form shadowed in the water. The effect is of poise and comprehension—a literal grasp of all that is.

Wordsworth has been accused of taking refuge in a reckless magniloquence, mere dimness and fog, when faced with large issues. This is a just criticism, and it is for the most part Wordsworth's own fault that it has been too liberally applied; for he is overbold to assume an understanding of his poetry's general quality, and a further readiness in the reader to relate the particular to the general: he wrote too much and too badly for his claims as to the imaginative unity of his life's work to be taken entirely seriously. Thus in two much quoted lines from *The Brothers*, he says:

The thought of death sits easy on the man
Who has been born and dies among the mountains.

As it stands, this will not do; but it is not written in Wordsworth's later vein of pastoral bombast. The

---

[1] *The Excursion*, Bk. IX. 437. For an early version of this passage see *The Prelude* (ed. de Selincourt), p. 562.

immediate context is of little help. The priest of a
mountain parish, when it is pointed out to him that the
graves in his churchyard are unmarked, replies:

> We have no need of names and epitaphs;
> We talk about the dead by our fire-sides.
> And then, for our immortal part! *we* want
> No symbols, Sir, to tell us that plain tale:
> The thought of death sits easy on the man
> Who has been born and dies among the mountains.

Wordsworth cannot mean that mountains symbolize
immortality because they are long lived: *The Brothers*
is a poem about universal change and decay, applied to
nature as to man. "Even among these rocks," he says,
you "can trace the finger of mortality":

> On that tall pike
> (It is the loneliest place of all these hills)
> There were two springs which bubbled side by side,
> As if they had been made that they might be
> Companions for each other: the huge crag
> Was rent with lightning—one hath disappeared;
> The other, left behind, is flowing still.
> For accidents and changes such as these
> We want not store of them;—a waterspout
> Will bring down half a mountain. . . .

Wordsworth fails to give notice of his real intention,
which is to refer to the mountain's place within his
greater landscape. He describes in *The Pedlar* how the
mountain appeared to his childhood both as an abiding
logic and as a history of sentient nature; and in *The
Prelude* he restates this as a double influence: he was
affected at once by their "forms perennial" and by
"the changeful language of their countenances".[1] The
mountains of his greater landscape speak with authority

---

[1] Bk. VII. 725.

of the passing and the permanent. But what they say is what they are: hence Wordsworth's fearful struggle with words, and especially with the verb "to be", as if to reach a linguistic fourth dimension in which the mountain-quality of time and eternity can be realized. And sometimes, as here, he attempts no more than a gesture towards his poetry's battle-field.

Another mention of immortality, similar to that in *The Brothers*, occurs in *The Prelude*, where Wordsworth speaks of the "imaginative impulse" which he received in the Alps from

> These forests unapproachable by death,
> That shall endure as long as man endures
> To think, to hope, to worship and to feel,
> To struggle, to be lost within himself
> In trepidation, from the blank abyss
> To look with bodily eyes and be consoled.[1]

Again he is not concerned with mere longevity: but the opaqueness of the passage leaves one undecided whether to take it at its face value, as incantation or as tiresome rant, as the case may be; or yet to suspend judgment. Later in the same book, Wordsworth returns to the immortality of forests. He relates how, as he travelled down the Simplon Pass, the features of the landscape impressed him as "the types and symbols of eternity"; and he names first:

> The immeasurable height
> Of woods decaying, never to be decay'd,
> The stationary blasts of water-falls. . . .

Forests are unapproachable by death because the seeds of life are nourished in their dying: to the mortality of life they oppose the vitality of death, and so Wordsworth can call them a consolation, and a type of eter-

---

[1] 1850, Bk. VI. 466.

nity. His thought here is very compact. In "the stationary blasts of waterfalls" the eternity theme is maintained and extended. As the forest is the type of life in death, so moving water is that of changeless change. This is fully and perfectly said in the last of the River Duddon Sonnets.

> I thought of Thee, my partner and my guide,
> As being passed away.—Vain sympathies!
> For, backward, Duddon! as I cast my eyes,
> I see what was, and is, and will abide;
> Still glides the Stream, and shall for ever glide;
> The Form remains, the Function never dies. . . .

In the case of the *Prelude* waterfalls, stillness in movement has a double force. There is the question of form and function just considered, and there is the genuine ambiguity of sense-experience; for, as Wordsworth says of another "foaming flood", moving water is "frozen by distance".[1] Thus "stationary blasts" contains stillness to the eye, the idea of form persisting through change, and a subtle undersense of function resting in the waterfall's eternal voice: whereas, in the Immortality Ode's "the cataracts blow their trumpets from the steep", the song has become dominant, while stillness and enduring form are gently admitted in the statuesque image of the cataract-trumpeter.

Wordsworth's greater landscape is therefore great indeed. Certainly there is nothing allegorical about this landscape: Wordsworth is in the strictest sense a nature poet, in suit of the natural world, eager to converse "with things that really are". But the sense of nature poet, although strict, is not confining. He can say with the Pedlar, "I see around me here Things which you cannot see"; and the poetry of solitude and relationship is his witness. In the eighth book of *The Prelude,* which

---

[1] *Address to Kilchurn Castle.*

he entitled *Retrospect*, his eye returns for a moment, as in the Immortality Ode, to the childhood scene,

> the Wilds
> In which my early feelings had been nursed—
> Bare hills and valleys, full of caverns, rocks,
> And audible seclusions, dashing lakes,
> Echoes and waterfalls, and pointed crags
> That into music touch the passing wind.

Here again are the landscape's primary features— wind, water, mountain, echo; and the strange abstract-concrete quality of "audible seclusions", alive to eye and ear and understanding.

III

THE POETRY OF INDECISION

THERE is a kind of courage in Wordsworth's treatment of his solitaries within their landscape
setting: he dares to trust his poetry to do its own work
in its own way, without reliance upon an alien intellectualism or relapse into the primary romantic vice of
vagueness and the cult of feeling. The Romantics themselves discussed this courage. Keats thought it a mark
of high genius, and pre-eminently Shakespearean, that
a man should be in deadly earnest about life and death,
and yet "capable of being in uncertainties, mysteries,
doubts, without any irritable reaching after fact and
reason"; "content with half-knowledge",[1] but with a
contentment opposed altogether to complacency. And
Coleridge, aware of a personal destiny of thought and
of a longing to escape it, was quick to condemn any
offering of the indefinite in substitution for the infinite.
Both were thinking of a balance, a moral integration,
hard to achieve and harder to maintain; and so was
Shelley, when he spoke of Wordsworth's power to
awaken thought-in-sense: while Wordsworth himself
used the language of the poetic memory and of the eye
made quiet, to describe the condition of passionate
serenity in which his best poetry was written.

There is a much smaller critical courage which can
make a study worthy of its subject; a complementary
faith in the power native to poetry. No major poet has
suffered so severely as Wordsworth from the growth of
the anthology habit. His effort is slow and cumulative:
the idea of the representative poem is in his case
peculiarly damaging; and the temptation to escape

[1] *Letters* (ed. Maurice Buxton Forman), p. 72.

from his poetry to some easier construction is for this
reason doubly hard to resist. The theme of Wordsworth's literalness is in fact a striving after critical
courage; for it seems to me much more false to the
quality of Wordsworth's imagination to brush aside the
landscape of

> I hear the Echoes through the mountains throng,
> The Winds come to me from the fields of sleep

in search of absent realities than to suppose, in the most
naïve way possible, that Wordsworth means what he
says. For if this second attitude is informed with the
devoted attention which Wordsworth asked for his
poetry, it may grow into understanding of his
meaning's unique immensity as it embraces an incarnate metaphysic of the natural world.

With characteristic bluntness Wordsworth asserted
that poetry must be "at once real and ideal" if it is to
achieve "truth in its largest sense"; an unremitting
discipline in "exact and accurate detail" that subor-
dinates itself "to the spirit of the whole".[1] But sub-
ordination is not sacrifice: there is no flight from literal
to metaphorical; but rather an evolution from within of
ampler, more inclusive, literalness. His poetry remains
a chronicle of things seen, however great its burden of
meaning, both with the solitary wanderers and the
primary features of his landscape, and with the
secondary figures: the cuckoo who is his own echo; the
glow-worm whose pinpoint light is both particular and
powerful; the rainbow-arch joining hope to memory;
the river "going and never gone"; the fish "that moves
And lives as in an element of death".

In one of his sonnets Wordsworth declares that "the
universe is infinitely wide". With its peculiar alliance
of narrowness and penetration his early poetry is saying

[1] Grosart, Vol. III. p. 488.

this all the time: in terms of an inspired monotony it finds within the world the answers to its questions, the realization of its potentialities, the passing of its limits. This concentration of effort to deny the finitude of nature is of course absent from Wordsworth's later poetry. There has been very general recognition of this change; and the traditional account of his decline from a healthy and confident religion of nature towards timid orthodoxy stands in loose relation to it—loose because it considers at once two issues that were better distinguished; that of poetry and joy and that of poetry and belief.

Wordsworth is partly responsible for the eagerness of critics to furnish a psychological explanation of his decline, for he was himself at pains to establish a necessary connexion between poetry and pleasure. This looms very large in the Preface to the *Lyrical Ballads*.

> The Poet writes under one restriction only, namely, the necessity of giving immediate pleasure to a human being. . . .

And if he is to give pleasure to others, the poet must himself be

> a man pleased with his own passions and volitions, and who rejoices more than other men in the spirit of life that is in him. . . .

In this respect Wordsworth never changed his mind. It remained a cardinal principle with him that only a happy man can write good poetry; and he attributed Coleridge's failure as a poet to his unhappiness, because of which "he could not afford to suffer with those whom he saw suffer".[1]

In speaking thus of Coleridge Wordsworth borrows from his own description of the Pedlar, which has about it a clear trace of autobiography:

[1] Barron Field's MS. *Memoirs*. Cited in *P.W.*, Vol. V. p. 413.

Unoccupied by sorrow or its own,
His heart lay open; and by nature tuned
And constant disposition of his thoughts
To sympathy with Man, he was alive
To all that was enjoyed where'er he went
And all that was endured; and in himself
Happy, and quiet in his cheerfulness,
He had no painful pressure from within[1]
Which made him turn away from wretchedness
With coward fears. He could afford to suffer
With those whom he saw suffer.[2]

At the end of *The Pedlar*, this theme of the poet's heart
lying open in delight and of "the constant disposition
of his thoughts To sympathy with man" is expanded
into a comprehensive philosophy of optimism. On its
own account a ramshackle affair, it is relevant to the
early poetry and to the decline of Wordsworth's middle
years.

In the form in which it was completed in 1798, *The
Pedlar* is a story of unrelieved distress concerning the
ruined cottage and its inhabitants. This story is subjected to a long reflective interpretation by the Pedlar,
who is himself the teller of the tale, in order that Wordsworth, his audience, shall "no longer read The forms
of things with an unworthy eye". The Pedlar's cheerful
argument is based on the Wordsworthian fact of the
mind's marriage to the natural world, its "quiet sympathies with things that hold An inarticulate language"; and it attempts to move from here to a further
sympathy, likewise inevitable, with man. "Once taught
to love such objects as excite No morbid passions", a
man "needs must feel The joy of that pure principle of

---

[1] *The Excursion* (l. 368) has "without"; but I think this must be the
mistake of Wordsworth and his editors, since "without" makes nonsense of
the familiar argument from inner to outer. The earliest version reads "within" (*P.W.*, Vol. V. p. 387).

[2] *P.W.*, Vol. V. p. 386.

love So deeply" that "he cannot choose But seek for
objects of a kindred love In fellow-natures".[1] By contemplating natural objects "in the relations which they
bear to man", we shall find that "all things shall speak
of man, and we shall read Our duties in all forms"; the
whole passage culminating in an outburst of Necessitarian optimism:

> Thus deeply drinking in the soul of things
> We shall be wise perforce, and we shall move
> From strict necessity along the path
> Of order and of good.[2]

The most striking thing about the Pedlar's meditation is its finality for Wordsworth. It reappears in 1814,
at a high point in *The Excursion's* argument,[3] substantially as it was written sixteen years before. And the
reason that Wordsworth had no more to say on this
subject cannot be that he had ceased to think about it
in the meantime, for the eighth book of *The Prelude*,
which cost him great effort and which he entitled *Love
of Nature Leading to Love of Man*, is vitally concerned
with it. *The Prelude* as a whole, with which must be
reckoned hundreds of lines of rationalistic verse
intended for *The Prelude* but finally not included,
affords ample evidence of his application. So does
Peter Bell, finished in 1798, but not published until
1819, after repeated and laborious revision.

The story of *Peter Bell* is simple, and in its method of
proceeding very significant. Peter is in the tradition of
wandering solitaries, but distinguished from the others
by the wickedness of his ways: he is cruel to animals
and to men—and, indeed, to women; for Wordsworth
includes in a solemn catalogue of his vices the fact that
"he had a dozen wedded wives". Now Peter is im-
moral because, although he lives in sight of nature,

[1] *P.W.*, Vol. V. p. 400.   [2] *Ibid.*, p. 402.
[3] Bk. IV. 1207-95.

there has not taken place the marriage of mind to the external world which is the source of morality:

> He roved among the vales and streams,
> In the green wood and hollow dell;
> They were his dwelling night and day,—
> But nature ne'er could find the way
> Into the heart of Peter Bell.

Wordsworth does not ask why nature should have failed in the particular case of Peter Bell: he simply records it as an unhappy accident that

> Nature could not touch his heart
> By lovely forms, and silent weather,
> And tender sounds. . . .

The point of this long and on the whole unsuccessful poem is that Peter becomes a moral man when nature finally manages to touch his heart. Wordsworth summarizes the issue thus, by means of a characteristic breath image:

> And now is Peter taught to feel
> That man's heart is a holy thing;
> And Nature, through a world of death,
> Breathes into him a second breath,
> More searching than the breath of spring.

There is a clear connexion between the morality of *Peter Bell* and the Pedlar's ragbag necessitarianism. In neither case are the intellectual outworks of Wordsworth's position in themselves important. He is day-labouring within a philosophical tradition of no consequence, and profoundly unchristian in its ignorance of sin and its lack of interest in the will as a moral instrument. But there is no question that Wordsworth earnestly believed that by "deeply drinking in the soul of things We shall be wise perforce"; and this belief is an effective presence within the poetic idea of sympathy which dominates the world of solitude and relationship. Peter Bell's coming to virtue is, as we have seen, a matter of the gradual increase of moral perception as nature begins to touch him: "his heart is opening more and more". And beyond the crude externality with which Peter's progress is described, this ruling and imaginative sympathy is just discernible.

Wordsworth's half-statement of his idea of sympathy is in the form of a paradox. If Peter can be brought into contact with the world about him, all will be well:

> Let good men feel the soul of nature,
> And see things as they are.

Yet in one sense he is seeing things as they are at the beginning of the poem.

> In vain, through every changeful year,
> Did Nature lead him as before;
> A primrose by a river's brim
> A yellow primrose was to him,
> And it was nothing more.

Thus there are two ways of seeing the same primrose, the second way no less literal than the first. Wordsworth's poetry is about this second way; and it is important to recognize that he believed in a necessary coincidence of the literal-poetic seeing of a primrose with morality and wisdom: for this belief nourished his poetry. He failed many times to prove that love of nature leads to love of man, but found a kind of poetic salvation in his striving. Much of Wordsworth's poetry, especially the pastoral and patriotic verse of his middle age, was written with a fatal facility—he admits somewhere that he threw off many a sonnet in an idle moment, and one may find a great deal of idleness among the 523 sonnets published by himself; but the poetry of sympathy made demands upon his personal resources which he could not meet simply by direction of the will. His letters during this period, Dorothy's *Journals*, the condition of his manuscripts: all point to intense conscious effort; and the poetry itself to an entire commitment in which strength of will is matched by keenness of appetite, and the creative spirit is both horse and horseman.

Love of neighbour and love of neighbourhood are inseparable issues: it was thus, through the idea of sympathy, that he expressed his belief in the relevance of poetry to life. Without this belief, his peculiar earnestness, the disposition of the whole man towards poetic effort, would not have been possible. For the quality of the response rested on the quality of the challenge: hence his hatred of mere aestheticism in poetic theory and his urgent concern with the morality of all great poetry, and especially of his own. He wished to be thought of "as a teacher or as nothing", to enter upon the scene of life and make men better. In some degree he was aware that his power to address himself to nature depended on his conviction as to the supreme importance of what was to be found there.

"Assent," Wordsworth wrote, "is power." But assent does not wait upon the will; and there is respect for its complexity in his awareness of present strength as a poet, no less than in his fear of future weakness. When he thought about these things, Wordsworth attended to childhood. His very newness to the world lends the child understanding. Nothing stays the same for him or happens twice: all experience is unique, and in appreciation of this he looks around him with unrelenting care. What Coleridge called "the film of familiarity", and Wordsworth "the regular action of the world", has not as yet blunted his perception or sated his appetite. The power to see, the clearsightedness granted, in *The Prelude* phrase, "to unaccustomed eyes", and the desire to see, are both present in the child. Childhood is the fact upon which Wordsworth's philosophy of natural good reclines, and childhood is the marriage in love of poetry and morals: for children live by the principle of sympathy, finding themselves while they search for their neighbours in nature, among all modes of being. Hence in *The Prelude* account of childhood, as in the *Lyrical Ballads* theorizing about art, the cardinal poetic-moral abstractions—Joy, Desire, Power, Belief—jostle one another ceaselessly.

Speaking of his own childhood, Wordsworth describes how he felt

> that calm delight
> Which, if I err not, surely must belong
> To those first-born affinities that fit
> Our new existence to existing things,
> And, in our dawn of being, constitute
> The bond of union betwixt life and joy.[1]

This partnership of relational appetite and relational achievement, as Wordsworth understands it, comes into being at the threshold of life and of poetry. It is founded upon joy, in accordance with the *Lyrical Ballads* doctrine that "we have no sympathy but what is propagated by pleasure"; and it yields to both child and poet the "sense of possible sublimity" without which a corresponding sense of creative urgency cannot be roused.

Wordsworth realized that the bond between his childhood and his poetry was unsafe, and that to rest his huge optimism upon it was to court disaster. "I see by glimpses now," he wrote, while still a young man, "when age comes on, May scarcely see at all"[2]: in the poetry of the Great Decade there is the foretaste of ruin to be encountered in a hopeless wasting war against the mustering forces of time. But Wordsworth had no other course. However false his generalizations about

[1] *The Prelude*, Bk. I. 580.
[2] *The Prelude*, Bk. XI. 338.

I

art and life, the derivation of his own poetry from a childhood state "that hath more power than all the elements" cannot be challenged. He reflects upon slow failure and the dwindling of his resources, as upon that assent which he calls power, with massive self-knowledge.

Much is said in *The Prelude* and the Immortality Ode about the difficulty of recovering childhood vision, of seeing the truth when increasingly beset with lies engendered by mere habit and the passing of years. It is a very large difficulty, because it embraces capacity and desire: Wordsworth's frequent talk of power in connexion with childhood has as much moral as poetic reference. In the Immortality Ode he is primarily concerned with the child as poet born, with an under-theme of natural morality—the "brightness", we have seen, is "innocent". In the *Ode to Duty*, written towards the close of the Great Decade, there is a significant shift of emphasis: Wordsworth's principal interest is moral, but with backward glancing towards "the genial sense of youth", and the state of poetic splendour in which

> love is an unerring light,
> And joy its own security.

In these two odes he reviews his loss in both its aspects.

Wordsworth's final and most full discussion of this loss appears in the last book of *The Excursion*, which he doubtless intended to be the philosophical climax of the whole. The book opens with an abrupt statement of his doctrine of sympathy.

> "To every Form of being is assigned,"
> Thus calmly spoke the venerable Sage,
> "An *active* principle. . . ."

This principle "subsists In all things, in all natures", and, because of it, "Whate'er exists hath properties

that spread Beyond itself"—a truth of particular force
in the case of

> the human Mind,
> Its most apparent home. The food of hope
> Is meditated action; robbed of this
> Her sole support, she languishes and dies.
> We perish also; for we live by hope
> And by desire; we see by the glad light
> And breathe the sweet air of futurity;
> And so we live, or else we have no life.

The active or sympathetic principle, the urge in
everything to "spread beyond itself", Wordsworth
describes in purely human terms as hope and desire;
and in the lines immediately following, he supports his
thesis by an appeal to childhood, to the condition of
two boys who have just appeared on *The Excursion's*
quasi-dramatic scene.

> Tomorrow—nay perchance this very hour
> (For every moment hath its own tomorrow!)
> Those blooming Boys, whose hearts are almost sick
> With present triumph, will be sure to find
> A field before them freshened with the dew
> Of other expectations;—in which course
> Their happy year spins round.

Because childhood is the living vindication of Wordsworth's principle, age seeks always to return. As so
often, this theme moves Wordsworth to the authentic
sublime: his verse starts out for a moment from the
wretched stuff surrounding it.

> Ah! why in age
> Do we revert so fondly to the walks
> Of childhood—but that there the Soul discerns
> The dear memorial footsteps unimpaired
> Of her own native vigour . . . ?

Now Wordsworth has reached the decisive step in his argument. He wishes next to show that despite its loss of childhood's relational power, age has virtues of its own. The querulous, fidgeting manner of his opening is ominous.

> Do not think
> That good and wise ever will be allowed,
> Though strength decay, to breathe in such estate
> As shall divide them wholly from the stir
> Of hopeful nature. Rightly it is said
> That Man descends into the VALE of years;
> Yet have I thought that we might also speak,
> And not presumptuously, I trust, of Age,
> As of a final EMINENCE; though bare
> In aspect and forbidding, yet a point
> On which 'tis not impossible to sit
> In awful sovereignty. . . .

Wordsworth calls age an eminence because he wishes to compare it with a mountain top. It is the experience of one who looks down upon the world from a high peak "in some placid day of summer" that

> the gross and visible frame of things
> Relinquishes its hold upon the sense,
> Yea almost on the Mind herself, and seems
> All unsubstantialized. . . . For on that superior height
> Who sits, is disencumbered from the press
> Of near obstructions, and is privileged
> To breathe in solitude, above the host
> Of ever-humming insects, 'mid thin air
> That suits not them. The murmur of the leaves
> Many and idle, visits not his ear:
> This he is freed from, and from thousand notes
> (Not less unceasing, not less vain than these)
> By which the finer passages of sense
> Are occupied; and the Soul, that would incline
> To listen, is prevented or deterred.

And may it not be hoped, that, placed by age
In like removal, tranquil though severe,
We are not so removed for utter loss;
But for some favour, suited to our need?
What more than that the severing should confer
Fresh power to commune with the invisible world,
And hear the mighty stream of tendency
Uttering, for elevation of our thought,
A clear sonorous voice, inaudible
To the vast multitude; whose doom it is
To run the giddy round of vain delight,
Or fret and labour on the Plain below.

This is bad poetry, and in its kind of badness quite
unlike the work of Wordsworth's first maturity. It
attempts the serene and total vision of spiritual detachment: it achieves a gathering up of its skirts and a tiresome snobbery. In Wordsworth's own unhappy phrase,
it breathes "thin air"—air too thin for the poetry of
his own past, which was bound to hear the ever-
humming insects and the murmur of the leaves, now
together classed as "near obstructions", or it must have
died. "The mighty stream of tendency", the only
memorable thing here, has been saved from a notebook
fragment written in 1798.[1] Otherwise there is poverty,
and a rejection of all that made his early poetry rich.
This is at once evident in its distaste for close observation, and its railing at the senses. But behind this, and
much more important, is the crude opposition of "the
gross and visible frame" and "the invisible world".
Wordsworth is trying to write a new kind of poetry.
He can assent no longer to the literalness of the natural
order and its moral-poetic power: he cannot strive, with
effort unparalleled in English poetry, to see things as
they are. He is trying to write transcendental poetry, to
tell tales of the invisible world. To him this does not

[1] *Wordsworth's Prelude* (ed. de Selincourt), p. 548.

appear a matter of choice. Age has come upon him as a
"removal" and a "severing", and he has no other
world to tell of. But the new discipline, which is no
less severe than the old, gives him much pain in the
learning.

Wordsworth's poetry was not suddenly invaded by
the spiritual and the transcendent. *The Excursion* was
published in 1814, but alteration is already to be seen
in *The Prelude*, finished nine years earlier. When the
childhood incidents of *The Prelude's* opening are held
against the desperately obscure idea of spiritual love
with which it concludes, the contrast is very striking:
or when Wordsworth's description, in the first book,
of his earliest intercourse

> Not with the mean and vulgar works of Man,
> But with high objects, with enduring things,
> With life and nature. . . .[1]

is compared with the final lines of the poem. "What
we have loved," he says, speaking of Coleridge and
himself,

> Others will love; and we may teach them how;
> Instruct them how the mind of man becomes
> A thousand times more beautiful than the earth
> On which he dwells, above this frame of things
> (Which, 'mid all revolution in the hopes
> And fears of men, doth still remain unchanged)
> In beauty exalted, as it is itself
> Of substance and of fabric more divine.

In this conclusion the mind's marriage "to this goodly
universe In love and holy passion" has suffered an
almost Platonic divorce.

The Prelude has a false continuity which obscures
this great change. When Wordsworth said, at the out-

[1] l. 435.

set, that his object was to "give pictures of Nature, Man and Society", he chose his words advisedly; for *The Prelude* was not conceived as a poem of epic growth and movement. It is a selection of distinct incidents, and its superiority over *The Excursion* is partly due to the fact that the autobiographical thread on which they are strung is much more serviceable than the dramatic. Attentive reading of *The Prelude* reveals how an alien consecutiveness, both in chronology and logic, has been imposed upon it—a conclusion supported by the external facts of its composition.

Wordsworth's work at the poem falls into two periods. During 1798 and 1799 he wrote the first two books, substantially as they appear in the 1805 text; and much more that was finally incorporated in later books. There follows a long interval of about four years, during which he scarcely touched the poem. Early in 1804 he resumed work, and finished the whole in the early summer of 1805.

The Prelude of 1798-9 is in the high tradition of solitude and relationship. The Discharged Soldier, who finds his place eventually in Book IV, has already been considered with the Wordsworthian solitaries; and he is the greatest among many. And *The Prelude* incidents, by epic standards an inert pile, a mere addition, are related, in a way which makes it proper to talk of Wordsworth as a philosophical poet, to the master-thesis of the mind's marriage to the world. The childhood episodes which crowd the first two books, and which are scattered throughout the rest of *The Prelude*, all expound the world's ministry through "intercourse with beauty" and "the impressive discipline of fear" (so that Wordsworth speaks of himself as "fostered alike by beauty and by fear"), and the mind's reciprocal action in human sympathy and appetite.

The Prelude of 1804-5 is a very different thing. Its quality cannot be caught at once because in the inter-

vening years a vital concentration has been lost, and in
its place there is dispersal of effort. Much of this later
Prelude is mere joinery, and often none too neat. Thus
in Book XI, two famous episodes, that of Wordsworth's
coming upon a gibbet in a lonely valley and that of his
waiting in a storm to be fetched home from school, are
linked by a bridge-passage which betrays its modest
function quite clearly:

> Yet another
> Of these to me affecting incidents
> With which we will conclude.[1]

The passages from the 1798-9 *Prelude* stand out in
brilliant contrast to their drab surroundings in the later
books.

The main task of the 1804-5 *Prelude* is to impress
clearly the autobiographical form and martial into con-
sequential argument "the history of a poet's mind".
For when Wordsworth wrote the earliest of *The Prelude*
episodes he had no thought of an independent poem
about his own past: these were related in their distinctness to the scheme of the philosophical *Recluse*. Even
when he returned to *The Prelude* in 1804, Wordsworth
imagined it in nothing like its final state. By this time
he had come to regard it as separate from *The Recluse*,
but intended it to contain only five books as against
the thirteen of the 1805 text. And so the later *Prelude*
was both planned and written during the next eighteen
months.

Change is perhaps most striking when the context
remains familiar. In Book VIII there is a very typical
solitary, a shepherd encountered in mountain mist.

> Seeking the raven's nest, and suddenly
> Surpriz'd with vapours, or on rainy days
> When I have angled up the lonely brooks
> Mine eyes have glanced upon him, few steps off,

[1] l. 343.

In size a giant, stalking through the fog,
His Sheep like Greenland Bears; at other times
When round some shady promontory turning,
His Form hath flash'd upon me, glorified
By the deep radiance of the setting sun:
Or him have I described in distant sky,
A solitary object and sublime,
Above all height! like an aerial Cross,
As it is stationed on some spiry Rock,
Of the Chartreuse, for worship.[1]

The shepherd is at first marked with obstinate peasant honesty, a "few steps off"—nobody can doubt it: and likewise his sheep. In the "Greenland bears" one discovers a gauche but convincing appeal to the unfamiliar the near-fabulous, to describe what was so strange and yet was clearly seen. About the shepherd looming gigantic in the mist there is a terrestrial sublimity worthy of the early *Prelude*. But after the sixth line Wordsworth loses his command. The description becomes rosily transcendental; the verse assumes the hazy, the golden, the remote, which is the conventional dress of otherness. Perhaps Wordsworth thought that he could make the shepherd "above all height" outshine the shepherd "few steps off". Or he may have mistrusted himself; so that his final unlucky reference to the Cross is a cry for help, in work which his poetry cannot do alone.

There is another solitary in the later *Prelude*, quite unlike the shepherd. In the midst of a London crowd, wholly occupied with his own thoughts, Wordsworth tells how

                                        lost
Amid the moving pageant, 'twas my chance
Abruptly to be smitten with the view
Of a blind Beggar, who, with upright face,

[1] l. 396.

Stood propp'd against a Wall, upon his Chest
Wearing a written paper, to explain
The story of the Man, and who he was.
My mind did at that spectacle turn round
As with the might of waters, and it seem'd
To me that in this Label was a type
And emblem, of the utmost that we know,
Both of ourselves and of the universe;
And, on the shape of the unmoving man,
His fixèd face and sightless eyes, I look'd
As if admonish'd from another world.[1]

In this case there is no descent into the mock sublime.
The passage falters for a moment in its unnecessary
explicitness as to the significance of the label; but with
"the shape of the unmoving man, His fixèd face and
sightless eyes", it recovers the characteristic spare
strength of its opening, reminiscent, in the details of
its phrasing—"upright face", "stood propp'd", "the
story of the man, and who he was"—, of the Discharged
Soldier himself. But it is distinguished from the early
Prelude by the air of profound unease that hangs over
it. All the great solitaries are ominous: none of them, as
this blind beggar, inauspicious. Wordsworth's encounter with him is instinct with defeat; and it
expresses well his entire attitude to the city, which is
very important in the later *Prelude* as an image of
sovereign chaos.

The London beggar illustrates a general truth, that
Wordsworth's achievement is most considerable when
he is entirely honest about the change he has experienced. This account is faithful to the personal tradition
—Wordsworth sees the beggar as he has always seen
his solitaries; but he cannot relate his vision, as once he
could, to the original scheme of *The Recluse*. The
optimism of the early *Prelude* is in the bone of the thing,

[1] Bk. VIII. 608.

inseparable from its conception and its execution. That of the late *Prelude* is a determined end towards which the poem must be manipulated, like the plot of a bad play. Wordsworth says, very near its conclusion, that *The Prelude* is a

> Song, which like a lark
> I have protracted, in the unwearied Heavens
> Singing, and often with more plaintive voice
> Attempted to the sorrows of the earth;
> Yet centring all in love, and in the end
> All gratulant if rightly understood.[1]

The last line gives itself the lie. One catches sight of Wordsworth already grown weary of his work, rushing through the last two books in a mere fortnight, with his brother three months dead and very much in mind. He records his feelings in a letter.

> I have the pleasure to say that I finished my poem about a fortnight ago. I had looked forward to the day as a most happy one; and I was indeed grateful to God for giving me life to complete the work, such as it is: but it was not a happy day for me; I was dejected on many accounts; when I looked back upon the performance it seemed to have a dead weight about it, the reality so far short of the expectation; it was the first long labour that I had finished, and the doubt whether I should ever live to write *The Recluse*, and the sense which I had of this poem being so far below what I seemed capable of executing, depressed me much; above all, many heavy thoughts of my poor departed Brother hung upon me, the joy which I should have had in showing him the Manuscript, and a thousand other vain fancies and dreams.[2]

At its best the late *Prelude* is urgently bewildered; torn between old certainties and new doubts, self-consuming in its efforts to deal justly with both. Only

---

[1] Bk. XIII. 380.
[1] *Early Letters* (ed. de Selincourt), p. 497.

once does it make its predicament entirely clear, and
then, as seems to me significant, by way of nightmare.
Wordsworth describes how he was reading Cervantes
by the sea, and, having fallen asleep, dreamed strangely.
In his dream Wordsworth was looking fearfully about
him in a sandy desert, when there appeared a mysterious figure riding on a dromedary, half Bedouin Arab,
half Don Quixote himself. The stranger was carrying a
stone under one arm, and under the other a shell; and
he explained that the stone was geometry and the shell,
"something of more worth", poetry. Wordsworth put
his ear to the shell and heard a voice, eloquent and
passionate, "in an unknown tongue, Which yet I
understood", foretelling the world's destruction by
flood. The other then told him that the stone spoke
certain truth, and that he himself was setting out to
bury both stone and shell against the deluge:

> The one that held acquaintance with the stars,
> And wedded soul to soul in purest bond
> Of reason, undisturbed by space or time;
> The other that was a god, yea many gods,
> Had voices more than all the winds. . . .

Wordsworth sought to remain with his companion.

> Far stronger, now, grew the desire I felt
> To cleave unto this man; but when I prayed
> To share his enterprise, he hurried on
> Reckless of me. . . .

And the dream ends thus:

> His countenance, meanwhile, grew more disturbed;
> And, looking backwards when he looked, mine eyes
> Saw, over half the wilderness diffused,
> A bed of glittering light: I asked the cause:
> "It is," said he, "the waters of the deep
> Gathering upon us"; quickening then the pace
> Of the unwieldy creature he bestrode,

He left me: I called after him aloud;
He heeded not; but, with his twofold charge
Still in his grasp, before me, full in view,
Went hurrying o'er the illimitable waste,
With the fleet waters of a drowning world
In chase of him; whereat I waked in terror,
And saw the sea before me, and the book
In which I had been reading, at my side.[1]

Let no one be deceived by the Miltonic diction of
this passage. Wordsworth's command of quickening
pace, mounting terror, imminent eclipse, is altogether
personal. He sustains magnificently the nightmare
twilight of the scene: only "the unwieldy creature", a
lapse very much in character, is false to it. And judgment as to diction may itself be overeasy; for neither
Milton, nor any miltonizer, could have written "the
fleet waters of a drowning world". But I quote Wordsworth's dream for its wider reference, for its dying
upon an all-embracing question, with Wordsworth a
mere spectator unable to influence the issue. The dream
looks back across the Great Decade towards *The Pedlar*,
in which Wordsworth first declared the alliance of
mathematics and the natural world, of reason and
experience. Mathematics and poetry are still related,
and with the intensity of dream-conviction. How
related, is now lost to waking sense; but they must be
saved together, though the attempt prove vain and
Wordsworth no party to it. Only in "the heroic attitudes of a dream" might a universal and an entirely
private distress become thus identified.

Wordsworth reacts to this new perplexity by
reducing the compass of *The Prelude*. He becomes
much more attentive to the surface narrative: many
hundreds of lines describing his residence in London

---

[1] 1850, Bk. V. 89. In the 1805 text Wordsworth gives the dream, quite
unplausibly, to a friend.

or his part in the French Revolution have nothing but
the sequence of events between themselves and complete destitution. The limiting of imaginative scope is
betrayed by his persistent stating of his terms of
reference, as if to avoid wider and undesired consequences. Thus there is a false and restricting finality
in the later *Prelude's* attitude to the opposition of
countryside and city, as the types of natural and arti-
ficial. But the first indication of this and of other
changes is to be found in the work of the four years
dividing the early from the late *Prelude*.

In *Michael*, as we have seen, Wordsworth opposes
the country and the town. But the part played by the
town is quite unimportant: it is the occasion of inexplicable ruin, serving only to emphasize the poem's
cyclical movement, and the solitary's return, after
disaster has struck him down, to the scene of its
opening. *Michael* is a successful poem about solitude
and relationship: the solitary and the natural scene are
honestly regarded in the light of a structural optimism
that seeks to contain suffering, and not to exclude or
deny it. All that has passed is gathered up in the
principle of sympathy, in "the strength of love" manifested in Michael's care for his sheep and attention to
the wind. But this dichotomy of town and country is
none the less menacing: it threatens the seriousness
with which Wordsworth strove to make his poetry "the
acknowledged voice of life". For as the writing of
poetry became more difficult and painful, so the temptation to ease the burden grew harder to resist. And he
had here the means at hand. The life of the city, described in *The Prelude* as "by nature an unmanageable
sight", might be required, even though unconsciously,
to contain all that poetic experience itself found most
hard to manage. Wordsworth's attitude to the city

matters very little: it is of purely negative significance that he found this the way to dispose silently of embarrassment. But the effect on the poetry of the country is all-important. Thus opposed to the town, the greater landscape is a thing of diminished urgency and comprehension. Wordsworth became able to say less, and he had less to say—thus the complexity of decline. Even when he addressed himself to poetry as to a total activity, he was thinking, do what he might, of a reduced totality. And often he was consciously satisfied with less.

1800, the year of *Michael*, is also the year of *Home at Grasmere*, the first book of *The Recluse* and the only part of it that Wordsworth ever finished. The theme of *Home at Grasmere* is Wordsworth's retirement to Dove Cottage with Dorothy, to live the good life and to write poetry. Town and country are once more contrasted, in terms of the first principles of Wordsworth's poetic philosophy. Grasmere is the scene of solitude-in-relationship sustained through sympathy; the city, of false solitude or isolation, of meaningless difference and meaningless identity, loveless and unintelligible. Wordsworth describes the entire society of birds, beasts and men, in their successive generations, and the companionship of surrounding hills:

> Say boldly then that solitude is not
> Where these things are: he truly is alone,
> He of the multitude whose eyes are doomed
> To hold a vacant commerce day by day
> With objects wanting life, repelling love;
> He by the vast Metropolis immured,
> Where pity shrinks from unremitting calls,
> Where numbers overwhelm humanity,
> And neighbourhood serves rather to divide
> Then to unite.[1]

[1] *P.W.*, Vol. V. p. 333.

The argument of the later *Prelude* is here neatly epi-
tomized. And against the city stands Grasmere,

> A Whole without dependence or defect,
> Made for itself. . . .[1]

Much of *Home at Grasmere* is written with fine care;
and in its approach to "the calmest, fairest spot of
earth", shiningly gentle. But it is altogether smaller
poetry; restrictedly Paradisal, seeking Grasmere too
exclusively for retreat and shelter. One may observe
Wordsworth drawing his pencil round the manageable,
though still capable of greater range.

> What want we? have we not perpetual streams,
> Warm woods, and sunny hills, and fresh green fields,
> And mountains not less green, and flocks, and herds,
> And thickets full of songsters, and the voice
> Of lordly birds, an unexpected sound
> Heard now and then from morn till latest eve,
> Admonishing the man who walks below
> Of solitude, and silence in the sky?[2]

As if to admit the untruth of any circumscribed
perfection, Wordsworth says that he is forced, even in
Grasmere,

> To cast from time to time a painful look
> Upon unwelcome things, which unawares
> Reveal themselves. . . .[3]

But the poem's quality is not to be altered by a saving
clause. The circle of self-sufficiency is drawn in the
first place round the whole vale of Grasmere; then, in
case this outer defence should be surrendered to the
world, round the poet's own household at Dove
Cottage:

[1] *P.W.*, Vol. V. p. 318.
[2] *Ibid.*, p. 317.
[3] *Ibid.*, p. 329.

And if this
Were otherwise, we have within ourselves
Enough to fill the present day with joy,
And overspread the future years with hope,
Our beautiful and quiet home. . . .[1]

And finally round the poet's individual genius, by
virtue of the "something within which yet is shared by
none".[2] Despite its obvious accomplishment, *Home at
Grasmere* points the way beyond Wordsworth's own
decline, to an entire tradition of latter-day pastoral.

This change is sadly reflected in the disassociation of
his poetry's landscape and his poetry's morality.
Wordsworth always had a weakness for overt moralizing: even in *Tintern Abbey*, one of the greatest of the
landscape poems, there is the Boy-Scoutishness of the
"little, nameless, unremembered, acts Of kindness",
unworthy of the theme of spiritual presences and their
sustaining power. And as his early strength began to
ebb, this tendency became ever more apparent, the
landscape of his poetry being now too small to manifest
the moral quality of life through its expression of life's
physical context. Hence the opposition, blunt and con-
fined like that of town and country, of human life and
its natural setting. Already in *Home at Grasmere*
Wordsworth shows an unwonted eagerness to establish
an explicit moral connexion between the vale and those
who live there. There is a mood, he says, of forgetful-
ness and pleasant self-deception, which can

bear us on
Without desire in full complacency,
Contemplating perfection absolute
And entertained as in a placid sleep.[3]

This is a state in which "the Soul becomes, Words
cannot say, how beautiful"; and Wordsworth, once

[1] *P.W.*, Vol. V. p. 335.   [2] *Ibid.*, p. 336.   [3] *Ibid.*, p. 324.
K

caught up in it, attains the vision of Grasmere and its inhabitants in perfect harmony.

> They who are dwellers in this holy place
> Must needs themselves be hallowed, they require
> No benediction from the Stranger's lips,
> For they are blest already. None would give
> The greeting "peace be with you" unto them,
> For peace they have, it cannot but be theirs,
> And mercy and forbearance.

Aware that this dream-picture will not suffice, Wordsworth at once denies that he came to Grasmere "betrayed by tenderness of mind That feared, or wholly overlooked the truth". On the contrary:

> I came not dreaming of unruffled life,
> Untainted manners; born among the hills,
> Bred also there, I wanted not a scale
> To regulate my hopes. Pleased with the good,
> I shrink not from the evil with disgust,
> Or with immoderate pain.

He then proceeds to moderate his claims:

> Yet is it something gained, it is in truth
> A mighty gain, that Labour here preserves
> His rosy face, a Servant only here
> Of the fire-side, or of the open field,
> A Freeman, therefore, sound and unimpaired,
> That extreme penury is here unknown. . . .

And so on. But Wordsworth cannot leave the subject alone. He comes back to it, after a discreet interval, and restates the impossible perfection of his first vision, in scarcely milder terms.

> Take we at once this one sufficient hope,
>   . . . that, feeling as we do
> How goodly, how exceeding fair, how pure
> From all reproach is yon etherial vault,

And this deep Vale, its earthly counterpart,
By which, and under which, we are enclosed
To breathe in peace, we shall moreover find
(If sound, and what we ought to be ourselves,
If rightly we observe and justly weigh)
The Inmates not unworthy of their home
The Dwellers of their Dwelling.[1]

In this respect also, *Home at Grasmere* anticipates decline. The particular small moral preoccupation, the direct assault upon the understanding that advertises its intention and excites resistance, are indications of ill omen. Keats states the case against this kind of poetry with force and with justice.

It may be said that we ought to read our contemporaries—that Wordsworth &c. should have their due from us. But, for the sake of a few fine imaginative or domestic passages, are we to be bullied into a certain Philosophy engendered in the whims of an Egotist—Every man has his own speculations, but every man does not brood and peacock over them till he makes a false coinage and deceives himself. Many a man can travel to the very bourne of Heaven, and yet want confidence to put down his half-seeing. Sancho will invent a Journey heavenward as well as any body. We hate poetry that has a palpable design upon us—and if we do not agree, seems to put its hand in its breeches pocket. Poetry should be great and unobtrusive, a thing which enters into one's soul, and does not startle it or amaze it with itself, but with its subject.[2]

In one sense Wordsworth thought too much, and in another sense he did not think enough. He ruined his poetry in the effort to give it intellectual point and to make it serve an immediate moral purpose: at the same time he grew afraid of reasoning through to the end, poetically. Keats has it again, when he remarks of a

---

[1] *P.W.*, Vol. V. p. 334.
[2] *Letters* (ed. Maurice Buxton Forman), p. 96.

particular poem, though with beautiful relevance to the wider issue, that "it is a kind of sketchy intellectual Landscape—not a search after Truth".[1] The fate that overtakes the landscape of Wordsworth's early poetry could not be better summarized: its loss of depth and width and detail, its sacrifice of the universal and the particular for the merely general.

Two more landscape poems, *Hart-Leap Well* and *The Brothers*, were written in the watershed year of 1800, while *The Prelude* slept. *Hart-Leap Well* is about the death of a hart who threw himself down from a cliff, in his great distress, after he had been hunted for many hours. Nothing will grow at the place he died, nor will animals come to drink there. This story of innocent suffering is treated in two ways. A shepherd who has just related it to Wordsworth does not ask why such things should happen under Heaven: instead, he wonders what made the hart choose this very place to die.

> For thirteen hours he ran a desperate race;
> And in my simple mind we cannot tell
> What cause the Hart might have to love this place,
> And come to make his death-bed near the well.

It may be that he died where he was born:

> And he perhaps, for aught we know, was born
> Not half a furlong from that self-same spring.
>
> Now, here is neither grass nor pleasant shade;
> The sun on drearier hollow never shone;
> So will it be, as I have often said,
> Till trees, and stones, and fountain, all are gone.

And Wordsworth then replies:

> Grey-headed Shepherd, thou hast spoken well;
> Small difference lies between thy creed and mine:

---

[1] *Letters* (ed. Maurice Buxton Forman), p. 56.

This Beast not unobserved by Nature fell;
His death was mourned by sympathy divine.

The Being, that is in the clouds and air,
That is in the green leaves among the groves,
Maintains a deep and reverential care
For the unoffending creatures whom he loves.

Wordsworth is wrong: there is a world of difference between the two creeds. The poet puts the direct
question which the shepherd left unasked, and tries to
meet the fact of suffering with an assertion of God's, or
Nature's, loving care. This may be the truth; but God's
love for the murdered creature is still too difficult a thing
to be stated thus. Another's love must be expressed to
be experienced, and, if from God, must enfold hart and
hound and horseman. There is a false neatness about
Wordsworth's implied question and answer—too much
and too little thought—which no banging the big Pantheistic drum can make acceptable. We resist it, as
poetry "that has a palpable design upon us".

The shepherd says something which cannot be called
a creed at all, in the sense of Wordsworth's own statement. He suggests that the hart suffered for thirteen
hours in order to meet his end at his beginning. Wordsworth looks for the solution to a puzzle: the shepherd is
halted by the fact of long pursuit and death at this place.
In wondering why the hart died *here*, he neither answers
nor evades what must seem the larger question: somehow he illuminates its circumstances, so that it looks
different, in a way bearable; yet is still a question. Perhaps, as he ran, the hart held a remembered landscape
before his eyes, and at the last, material and immaterial
came together. The idea of return in extremity to the
familiar scene reflects honestly the way in which
Wordsworth had been trying all his life to understand
the world. In the most serious of his schoolboy poems,
he says:

> Dear native regions, I foretell,
> From what I feel at this farewell,
> That, wheresoe'er my steps may tend,
> And whensoe'er my course shall end,
> If in that hour a single tie
> Survive of local sympathy,
> My soul will cast the backward view,
> The longing look alone on you.[1]

These blundering steps led him eventually to the poetry of solitude and relationship, to the powerful and familiar landscapes of *Tintern Abbey* and *Michael*. *Hart-Leap Well* does not explain suffering and death any more than *Tintern Abbey* explains absence and change; but what is unexplained by these poems does not remain unaffected.

The Brothers, like *Michael*, is a blank-verse dramatic poem of nearly five hundred lines. As in *Michael* and the other poems of 1800, a landscape is recovered. Once again it is a painful story, and painful with new emphasis; for the pain's insolubility becomes almost the theme of the poem. A man returns after many desperate years to his native valley, and finds his brother dead and even the mountains and rivers of his childhood altered by the violence of nature. The priest of the place, who now does not recognize him, urges that he should remain:

> The other thanked him with an earnest voice;
> But added, that, the evening being calm,
> He would pursue his journey. So they parted.
>
> It was not long ere Leonard reached a grove
> That overhung the road: he there stopped short,
> And, sitting down beneath the trees, reviewed
> All that the Priest had said: his early years
> Were with him:—his long absence, cherished hopes,

[1] *Dear Native Regions*. See *P.W.*, Vol. I. p. 281, for the early version.

And thoughts which had been his an hour before,
All pressed on him with such a weight, that now,
This vale, where he had been so happy, seemed
A place in which he could not bear to live:
So he relinquished all his purposes.

Wordsworth regarded his own brother's death, in
1805, as the cause of profound alteration in himself: it
is the "great distress", which, as he says in the poem
about Peele Castle, "hath humanized my soul"; and
which leads him to "welcome fortitude, and patient
cheer, And frequent sights of what is to be borne". The
crisis was real enough, but not unheralded, since
nothing is altogether new in imagination; and *The
Brothers*, humane, gently despairing, grave and un-
emphatic, is the forerunner of much in Wordsworth's
later poetry that is by no means meritless, although unlike what has gone before. This is the poetry of will,
as opposed to the poetry of intellect. It has no palpable
design upon us: indeed, but for a vision grown grey
with doubt, it would never have been written. It stands
out in welcome contrast to bad preaching and worse
philosophy because it remains true to the old and literal
way, in its endeavour to see things as they are. Certainly
it is much smaller poetry, lacking the metaphysical
passion that once directed Wordsworth in his search
for the second and revelatory sight of Peter Bell's
yellow primrose. But it is strong in its honesty: there
is no pretending that things make sense, and no pointing of a moral. The reader who wants a message must
extract it for himself from the unadvertised resolve and
discipline of its manner.

The other thanked him with an earnest voice;
But added, that, the evening being calm,
He would pursue his journey.

In the course of time Wordsworth grew more calcu-
lating in his attitude to the poetry of will. The *Ode to*

Duty, and his discussion of "the years that bring the philosophic mind" in the Immortality Ode, are quite consciously referred to the problem of decline: they ask what must be done when the light of childhood is extinguished. Wordsworth's answer betrays his own uncertainty. In the decade between the Immortality Ode and the publication of *The Excursion* he says a great deal about the need for Christian faith, and as much again about the human solution: about patient nursing of the will and husbanding of "what remains behind", about looking for relief precisely in one's humanity and in the "thoughts that spring Out of human suffering". Life is best undergone by him who does not ask too much of it. This is the period of Wordsworth's growing interest in Roman Stoicism: he came to know Seneca as he knew no philosopher, ancient or modern. And it is the period in which his own natural severity and detachment were much accentuated. The almost universal unkindness with which his early poetry was received only confirmed his belief in the fatal connexion of solitude and genius. He writes to a friend made anxious by the mockery and abuse showered on the *Poems in Two Volumes* published in 1807:

> Trouble not yourself upon their present reception; of what moment is that compared with what I trust is their destiny, to console the afflicted, to add sunshine to daylight by making the happy happier, to teach the young and the gracious of every age, to see, to think and feel, and therefore to become more actively and securely virtuous; this is their office, which I trust they will faithfully perform long after we (that is, all that is mortal of us) are mouldered in our graves.[1]

Two years later, in his open *Letter to Mathetes*, Wordsworth treats of present dishonour and isolation in

---

[1] *Letters*, 1806-11 (ed. de Selincourt), p. 126. Note the force of "therefore" in Wordsworth's argument.

wider terms, as the certain attendants of virtue. A man, he argues, must choose to follow the World or to follow Truth. The World entices him in many ways, but Truth

> does not venture to hold forth any of these allurements; she does not conceal from him whom she addresses the impediments, the disappointments, the ignorance and prejudice which her follower will have to encounter, if devoted, when duty calls, to active life; and if to contemplative, she lays nakedly before him a scheme of solitary and unremitting labour, a life of entire neglect perhaps, or assuredly a life exposed to scorn, insult, persecution, and hatred; but cheered by encouragement from a grateful few, by applauding conscience, and by a prophetic anticipation, perhaps, of fame—a late, though lasting consequence.

At its best this is a noble, if narrow, morality; a thing, as Wordsworth says in the same letter, of "passionate and pure choice", and sustained by "the inward sense of absolute and unchangeable devotion". Sometimes, it is true, he falls into a stiff-necked and very English stupidity, as in his *Character of the Happy Warrior*,

> Who, if he rise to station or command,
> Rises by open means, and there will stand
> On honourable terms, or else retire,
> And in himself possess his own desire;
> Who comprehends his trust, and to the same
> Keeps faithful with a singleness of aim;
> And therefore does not stoop, nor lie in wait
> For wealth, or honours, or for worldly state. . . .

The Happy Warrior is separated by whole continents from the *Ode to Duty*, next to which it stands in Wordsworth's own ordering of his poems. But they both illustrate, each according to its measure, the same aspect of Wordsworth's middle age.

I can therefore find no simple answer to the problem of Wordsworth's decline. What he says about the connexion between his childhood and his poetry is true, but still mysterious. I have tried to trace a dispersal of effort, in light pastoral, in the poetry of intellect and the poetry of will. To show what happened is not to give a reason; and I understand that my thesis must not be supposed to stand or fall by the loss of childhood and the advent of affliction. This would be an assumption as to the relation between literature and life no more warranted than that involved in any argument advancing, as the reason for decline, Wordsworth's love for Annette or for Dorothy, the failure of his eyesight or his political reaction. And yet it is a critic's business to show what happened. There was once an arrangement in Wordsworth's work, large and subtle enough to make him a very great poet. This was lost, and its place taken by the poetry of indecision. If the study of what happens in poetry were ever followed to a true conclusion, the reason for what happens—the critic no longer confusing natural causes and metaphysical reasons—would cease to perplex; not because it is a false question, but because it is here unaskable, as relating to a different order of the world.

Criticism of bad poetry has seldom saved itself from dullness, except through falsehood; and it would be a dishonest attempt to maintain interest, to pretend that the ways in which Wordsworth's early effort was dispersed can be precisely mapped. Much of his middle-aged poetry is bad just because it is unpredictable— random diversion-poetry that anybody might have written. But talk of tendencies is not quite idle.

The White Doe of Rylstone was written in 1807 and 1808, and published, by itself, in 1815. Except for *The Excursion*, it is the most ambitious work of Wordsworth's later life, a narrative poem of nearly two thousand lines, founded on a ballad in Percy's collec-

tion, *The Rising of The North*. It concerns the part
played by a single family, the Nortons, in the northern
revolt of 1569 against Queen Elizabeth, which had
first among its aims the restoring of the old religion.
Richard Norton is a fierce and aged squire, with nine
strong sons and a single daughter, Emily. Emily, in the
story's opening, is making a sacred banner at her
father's command, against the day of open insurrection.
She makes it unwillingly, because she has come,
through her mother's teaching, to profess Christianity
reformed. Francis, the eldest of Richard's sons, is also
against taking part in the revolt, but he fails to persuade
his father and brothers, who march off to war, bearing
Emily's banner with them. Francis foresees that the
whole family, and Rylstone Hall its home, are doomed
to perish in this adventure; and he makes Emily
promise to stay at Rylstone, doing—even hoping—
nothing, while he follows the others, unarmed and unobserved, to see what happens. The revolt fails: the
Nortons, except Francis, are captured and led off to
execution. Just before he dies, old Richard Norton
beseeches Francis to regain the banner if he can, and
bring it to Bolton Priory, to rest for ever there on St
Mary's shrine. Francis seizes the banner and escapes;
but before he can reach Bolton he is discovered by a
party of soldiers, and is killed.

Thus Emily survives alone, and the prophecy of
Francis is fulfilled. But not entirely, for he had not
reckoned with the white doe when, at the outset, he
foretold universal ruin:

> "The blast will sweep us all away—
> One desolation, one decay!
> And even this Creature!" which words saying,
> He pointed to a lovely Doe,
> A few steps distant, feeding, straying;
> Fair creature, and more white than snow!

"Even she will to her peaceful woods
Return, and to her murmuring floods,
And be in heart and soul the same
She was before she hither came:
Ere she had learned to love us all,
Herself beloved in Rylstone-hall."[1]

In fact the white doe does not leave, but remains with
Emily at the end of the poem, her consolation in sorrow
and companion in lonely wandering. And when she
dies, the white doe watches over her grave.

The white doe is the strangest figure in this difficult
poem. She belongs to Wordsworth's past: reciprocally
loving and loved, she is the latest of the relational solitaries. Her direct ancestors are the Lucy solitaries,
immaculate and ghostly, the Danish Boy, and the albatross of *The Ancient Mariner*, which Wordsworth
suggested to Coleridge when they were working together at the scheme of the poem, long ago in 1797.[2]
In the end, Coleridge placed the albatross at the centre
of a very unwordsworthian story of sin and nightmare-
horror and contrition: the other poet would not have
dealt like this with the white and lonely bird, moving
between sky and ocean. What he might have done at
the height of his powers is faintly suggested by the
entry of the doe, described ten years later:

—When soft!—the dusky trees between,
And down the path through the open green,
Where is no living thing to be seen;
And through yon gateway, where is found,
Beneath the arch with ivy bound,
Free entrance to the church-yard ground—
Comes gliding in with lovely gleam,
Comes gliding in serene and slow,
Soft and silent as a dream,
A solitary Doe!

[1] l. 554.   [2] Note to *We are Seven*, *P.W.*, Vol. I. p. 361.

> White she is as lily of June,
> And beauteous as the silver moon
> When out of sight the clouds are driven
> And she is left alone in heaven;
> Or like a ship some gentle day
> In sunshine sailing far away,
> A glittering ship, that hath the plain
> Of ocean for her own domain.[1]

There are several reasons why *The White Doe* is not one of Wordsworth's best poems. Like *The Lay of the Last Minstrel*, and unlike *Christabel*, it makes little more than period costume of the Antique Manner; and its cultivation of a light Spenserian Faery, though skilful, is too persistent. It is also overdeliberate in its following of Wordsworth's old ways. The doe is painstakingly white and solitary: whenever she appears, Wordsworth insists on her distinctness and radiancy, to show her "spotless, beautiful, innocent and loving",[2] in the language of his own comment on the poem. The emphasis on her relational function is even more crude. Once Emily and the doe are left alone, Wordsworth becomes absurdly anxious to reveal how perfect is their companionship in solitude. Emily is resting, after Francis has been killed, "with head reclined",

> When, with a noise like distant thunder,
> A troop of deer came sweeping by;
> And, suddenly, behold a wonder!
> For One, among those rushing deer,
> A single One, in mid career
> Hath stopped, and fixed her large full eye
> Upon the Lady Emily;
> A Doe most beautiful, clear-white,
> A radiant creature, silver-bright!

[1] l. 49.
[2] *Letters*, 1806-11 (ed. de Selincourt), p. 197.

Thus checked, a little while it stayed;
A little thoughtful pause it made;
And then advanced with stealth-like pace,
Drew softly near her, and more near—
Looked round—but saw no cause for fear;
So to her feet the creature came,
And laid its head upon her knee,
And looked into the Lady's face,
A look of pure benignity,
And fond unclouded memory.
It is, thought Emily, the same,
The very Doe of other years!—
The pleading look the Lady viewed,
And, by her gushing thoughts subdued,
She melted into tears—
A flood of tears that flowed apace
Upon the happy Creature's face.[1]

This day, says Wordsworth, was "the first of a re-
union Which was to teem with high communion", and
he continues, in much the same vein, to dwell upon
their love and understanding. Emily

hath ventured now to read
Of time, and place, and thought, and deed—
Endless history that lies
In her silent Follower's eyes;
Who with a power like human reason
Discerns the favourable season,
Skilled to approach or to retire,—
From looks conceiving her desire;
From look, deportment, voice, or mien,
That vary to the heart within.[2]

So that from this time until Emily's death, there might
the "kindliest intercourse ensue".
    No theme could have been more attractive to Words-

[1] l. 1639.   [2] l. 1714.

worth's young imagination than this one, of two different orders of nature perfectly alone and perfectly related. Nor is it handled, despite these damaging examples, without traces of his early mastery: the shining and unsexual quality of the relationship—light without heat—is reminiscent of the Lucy poems. To this extent Wordsworth still appears unselfconscious in his appreciation of the kind of poetry he writes; for he declines to versify the story of Beauty and the Beast, not long after he has written *The White Doe*, and with an interesting comment:

> I confess there is to me something disgusting in the notion of a human being consenting to mate with a beast, however amiable his qualities of heart. There is a line and a half in the *Paradise Lost* upon this subject which has always shocked me,—
>
> > "for which cause
> > Among the Beasts no Mate for thee was found."
>
> These are objects to which the mind ought not to be turned even as things in possibility.[1]

It can never have occurred to him, even "in possibility", that the love of Emily and the doe might be different from that which he imagines.

But *The White Doe* as a whole is all too self-aware: it manipulates solitude-in-relationship, as if to achieve the old result without expending the old effort. This very deliberation makes the poem strikingly intellectual; and Wordsworth himself stresses the mental nature of its tragedy. He believed that the poem would never be popular "because the main catastrophe was not a material but an intellectual one";[2] and he acknowledged that "the mere physical action was all unsuccessful",[3] averring at the same time that "the true

---

[1] *Letters*, 1806-11 (ed. de Selincourt), p. 427.   [2] *Ibid*., p. 197.
[3] *P.W.*, Vol. III. p. 548.

action" took place in the realm of spirit and intellect. The intellectual catastrophe of *The White Doe* is worth closer study for its relevance to the poet's own position.

The White Doe presents four parties in conflict—Protestant, Catholic, Stoic, and Relational-Solitary. Emily is unwilling to make the Catholic banner, and must be compelled, because she remembers her mother

> Who with mild looks and language mild
> Instructed here her darling Child,
> While yet a prattler on the knee,
> To worship in simplicity
> The invisible God, and take for guide
> The faith reformed and purified.[1]

Opposed to her is her father and the rebel cause, stated but not argued by Wordsworth, with a force quite new to his poetry, and premonitory of his late achievement:

> Might this our enterprise have sped,
> Change wide and deep the Land had seen,
> A renovation from the dead,
> A spring-tide of immortal green:
> The darksome altars would have blazed
> Like stars when clouds have rolled away;
> Salvation to all eyes that gazed,
> Once more the Rood had been upraised
> To spread its arms, and stand for aye.[2]

There is a kind of victory in defeat, when the old man, about to die, asks Francis to take the banner, and

> Bear it to Bolton Priory,
> And lay it on Saint Mary's shrine;
> To wither in the sun and breeze
> 'Mid those decaying sanctities.[3]

---

[1] l. 1036.   [2] l. 1261.   [3] l. 1292.

Francis stands between these two parties, and is distinct from both. The speech in which he bids farewell to Emily stems from the poetry of will and from Wordsworth's reading in Stoicism. He speaks of the consolation to be found in "unmerited distress"—"in that thy very strength must lie"; of the need to play one's part exactly and without fear in the great drama which is the world:

> Farewell all wishes, all debate,
> All prayers for this cause, or for that!
> Weep, if that aids thee; but depend
> Upon no help of outward friend;
> Espouse thy doom at once, and cleave
> To fortitude without reprieve.[1]

He continues in praise of the human virtues of "forbearance and self-sacrifice"; and his speech ends thus:

> Be strong;—be worthy of the grace
> Of God, and fill thy destined place:
> A Soul, by force of sorrows high
> Uplifted to the purest sky
> Of undisturbed humanity.[2]

The argument of Francis, though not expressly directed against the Christian elements of *The White Doe*, is none the less very unchristian. Emily is in fact aware of the gulf between his attitude and her own, for she implores her mother's pious ghost to "descend on Francis", and bid him

> beware
> Of that most lamentable snare,
> The self-reliance of despair![3]

But it is upon the clash of a humanistic philosophy of reason, will, and duty, and the love shared by Emily and the doe, that the intellectual catastrophe and the

---

[1] l. 540.   [2] l. 583.   [3] l. 1054.

L

spirituality of the poem's action chiefly depend. Emily resists the desire to follow her family to the war because she regards her brother's injunction as an "insuperable bar". Reluctantly she admits, in a paraphrase of his own last words to her, that

> *Her duty is to stand and wait;*
> In resignation to abide
> The shock, AND FINALLY SECURE
> O'ER PAIN AND GRIEF A TRIUMPH PURE.[1]

Emily makes half-hearted assent to his argument, which is itself no more than half justified by events.

> Behold the prophecy fulfilled,
> Fulfilled, and she sustains her part!
> But here her Brother's words have failed;
> Here hath a milder doom prevailed;
> That she, of him and all bereft,
> Hath yet this faithful Partner left;
> This one Associate that disproves
> His words, remains for her, and loves.[2]

This is the point of the poem. Francis was right to foretell disaster, and Emily's final mastery of pain. But he was also wrong; for hers is not the kind of victory he had expected. It is a victory in love, that "disproves his words".

The White Doe, then, invokes the old against the new, and in doing so expresses the personal dilemma. Wordsworth's past stands over against his present, and is felt to refute it; but Emily's victory, which is this refutation, can have no poetic interest unless the past returns full-nerved, to confront later time: her life with the doe is otherwise a paper triumph. And it is partly because Wordsworth cannot recover solitude-in-relationship, except through intellectual definition, that *The White Doe* is a failure.

.1069.   [2] l. 1783.

There is also the important difficulty that Wordsworth does not know—if he did, the poetry of indecision would not have been written—what he means by Emily's "triumph pure". If it were simply a matter of past confounding present, nature would finally be overcome by deeper nature. But there is a sudden loss of clarity at the end of *The White Doe*, when it becomes impossible to be certain whether Emily's victory is of earth or of heaven. Wordsworth echoes Francis, and lays the same stress on the natural, when he speaks of her as

> Uplifted to the purest sky
> Of undisturbed mortality.[1]

But this is a most equivocal mortality; for she is "by sorrow lifted toward her God", and she

> stood apart from human cares:
> But to the world returned no more. . . .[2]

She is stranger both to the mortal and immortal state, "faintly, faintly tied To earth", suspended and inert, the image of Wordsworth's impotence. Future is here involved, no less than past and present; and the movement towards a poetry of the supernatural.

[1] l. 1852.   [2] l. 1859.

IV

THE BAPTISED IMAGINATION

WORDSWORTH's high opinion of *The White Doe* and his insistence on its spirituality are closely connected. He thought the poem a complete failure in terms of its physical action, but made large claims for its other part, boasting, according to one story,[1] that he had published it in quarto "to show the world my own opinion of it", thus inviting comparison with the more fleshly romances of Scott and Byron which were also published in quarto. His own comments on *The White Doe* make it clear that he believed its spiritual success to lie in the relationship of Emily and the doe. He describes Emily as raised to "heights of heavenly serenity", as "ascending to pure etherial spirituality and forwarded in that ascent by communion with a creature not of her own species";[2] while the highest "point of imagination" in the poem is "nothing less than the Apotheosis of the Animal. . . ."[3] And again: "The anticipated beatification, if I may say so, of her mind, and the apotheosis of the companion of her solitude, are the points at which the Poem aims, and constitute its legitimate catastrophe, far too spiritual a one for instant or wide-spread sympathy. . . ."[4]

This talk of beatification and apotheosis, of the doe "raised from its mere animal nature into something mysterious and saint-like",[5] has a challenging novelty about it. Even the vocabulary would have been impossible ten years earlier. And Wordsworth's remarks

[1] Thomas Moore, *Memoirs*. Discussed by Miss Edith Batho, *The Later Wordsworth*, pp. 83-4 n.
[2] *Letters*, 1806-11 (ed. de Selincourt), p. 197.
[3] *Letters*, 1811-20 (ed. de Selincourt), p. 705.
[4] *P.W.*, Vol. III. p. 543.   [5] *Ibid.*, p. 548.

about his poem, agreeing too closely with each other for any possibility of accident, are accompanied by a more general observation which is also new and also deliberately made:

> Throughout, objects (the Banner, for instance) derive their influence not from properties inherent in them, not from what they are actually in themselves, but from such as are bestowed upon them by the minds of those who are conversant with or affected by those objects. Thus the Poetry, if there be any in the work, proceeds whence it ought to do, from the soul of Man, communicating its creative energies to the images of the external world.[1]

At one time Wordsworth believed that poetry and life were founded on the principle of reciprocity, on "ennobling interchange Of action from within and from without"; and in the giant *Recluse* he intended to demonstrate this truth. *The Recluse* was never finished, for a reason easier to confess than to comprehend: Wordsworth changed his mind. Already, in the last lines of *The Prelude*, the inner world is seen "above this frame of thing.... In beauty exalted". And now Wordsworth is urging that the interest of his poetry is spiritual, that the soul of man, instead of "working but in alliance with the works Which it beholds", is a single labourer.

As he suggests, the sacred banner is a key to this great change. Rivalling the doe herself in imaginative stature, the banner spans the action of the poem: bathed at its opening in Emily's tears, at its end in her brother's blood, throughout its central violence, the focus of Catholic effort. Francis, the hidden observer,

> following wheresoe'er he might,
> Hath watched the Banner from afar,
> As shepherds watch a lonely star,
> As mariners the distant light. . . .[2]

---

[1] *Letters*, 1811-20 (ed. de Selincourt), p. 705.   [2] l. 757.

and the banner becomes a guiding star not only for the Nortons but for the entire army. When old Richard Norton "took the Banner and unfurled The precious folds", the host rallied round him at once.

> "Uplift the Standard!" was the cry
> From all the listeners that stood round,
> "Plant it,—by this we live or die."
> The Norton ceased not from that sound,
> But said; "The prayer which ye have heard,
> Much injured Earls! by these preferred,
> Is offered to the Saints, the sigh
> Of tens of thousands, secretly."
> "Uplift it!" cried once more the Band,
> And then a thoughtful pause ensued:
> "Uplift it!" said Northumberland—
> Whereat, from all the multitude
> Who saw the Banner reared on high
> In all its dread emblazonry,
> A voice of uttermost joy brake out. . . .[1]

What Wordsworth means by influence bestowed on objects as opposed to influence within them becomes clear from his treatment of the banner. He has an important use for the distinction between that which a thing is and that which it stands for. Furled, it is a banner: unfurled, it is "the ransom of a sinful world", a divine ambassador by virtue of the thing depicted on it. Its meaning is then understood. And the ritual shout, thrice repeated, makes the raising of the banner a sacramental gesture. This dualism runs through the poem's action. Emily objects not to her labour in making the banner but to its significance; and Francis, who at first opposed a cramped intellectual argument to the whole adventure, dies trying to bring the banner home, impelled by motives both in and out of the world, almost Shakespearean in their complexity and pathos.

[1] l. 670.

Quite new in Wordsworth is this show of emblematic power, this grasping of otherness through thing and act. And if the banner and the white doe worked to-gether, instead of thwarting each other's purpose, the whole would not be a failure. As it is, the new poetry is an uncertain element in an unsuccessful poem, no more than an introduction to the problem of Words-worth's Christianity.

Encouraged by the existence of the rival texts of 1805 and 1850, students of Wordsworth's religion have often concerned themselves with *The Prelude*. But his alterations to the 1805 text make a poor basis for generalization: as a whole, they are unimportant and even misleading. Wordsworth practised a kind of theo-logical surgery on the body of his poem, grafting on to it pious digressions, and cutting away parts so dis-tempered as to offend sound doctrine. Sometimes this is done with a simple-hearted dexterity entertaining to observe, as when

> I worshipped them among the depths of things
> As my soul bade me. . . .
> I felt and nothing else[1]

in the 1805 text becomes, in 1850,

> Worshipping then among the depths of things
> As piety ordained. . . .
> I felt, observed, and pondered;

and when

> God and nature's single sovereignty[2]

is saved for orthodoxy in this fashion:

> Presences of God's mysterious power
> Made manifest in Nature's sovereignty.

[1] Bk. XI. 234.   [2] Bk. IX. 237.

There is no denying the evidence of these changes. Wordsworth grew sensitive to accusations of heresy, especially pantheistic, levelled against his work; and he resorted to unworthy expedients in order to refute them. This was a sad mistake: he would have been better employed writing new poems than patching old ones. And it was doubly unfortunate in that it has lent colour to the belief that Wordsworth's Christianity was a timid afterthought, a false gesture of respectability comparable with his toryism or his taste for the nobility or his acceptance of the Laureateship. Thus the picture of an unlovely, frigescent character has been built up and generally accepted, which, although by no means wholly false, is least true in the things that matter most.

Wordsworth's alteration to poems already written went much further than the trimming of obnoxious details. *Peter Bell* and *The Pedlar* are both test cases, since they were written early and published late, with ample time for reflection. *Peter Bell* is also a very simple test case, because it is the most direct of Wordsworth's poems in its approach to the relationship between mind and nature.[1] As the result of a deficiency in Peter himself, "nature ne'er could find the way Into the heart of Peter Bell". Wordsworth views the problem from the standpoint of nature and asks what must be done by her when the opposite and human term of the relation has failed to play its part: this is the "theme but little heard of among men" to which he refers in the Prospectus to *The Recluse;* not how the mind is fitted to the world, but how "the external world is fitted to the mind".

The poem suffers on account of this directness; for Nature becomes absurdly purposeful in her assault on Peter's heart. "Potent spirits" and "dread beings" are invoked, together with terrible sights and sounds,

[1] See pp. 115-7.

which were the Gothic apparatus of Wordsworth's own
schoolboy verse. Mindful of his present task, Wordsworth insists that none of these happenings are supernatural, thereby heightening their absurdity. A
"rumbling sound" that made Peter believe "that earth
was charged to quake And yawn for his unworthy sake"
was in fact

> by a troop of miners made,
> Plying with gunpowder their trade,
> Some twenty fathoms under ground.

But the distinction between natural and supernatural
agents of Peter's regeneration is not easily maintained.
Even in the early versions of the poem Wordsworth has
to call upon "a fervent methodist", encountered
"preaching to no unheeding flock", to assist nature in
her work. And many years later, shortly before he published *Peter Bell*, Wordsworth added two stanzas in
which he described a further influence on Peter,
effected through the donkey which he had stolen and
ill-treated.

> 'Tis said, meek Beast! that, through Heaven's grace,
> He not unmoved did notice now
> The cross upon thy shoulder scored,
> For lasting impress, by the Lord
> To whom all human-kind shall bow;
>
> Memorial of his touch—that day
> When Jesus humbly deigned to ride,
> Entering the proud Jerusalem,
> By an immeasureable stream
> Of shouting people deified.[1]

It is almost as if Grace and Nature were consciously
opposed, and the frailty of Nature admitted. These
added stanzas, fine in themselves, do not improve
Peter Bell: rather, they make matters worse by denying

[1] *P.W.*, Vol. II. pp. 377, 530.

momentarily and at a late stage the pagan optimism from which it proceeds. It is because they go to the root of Wordsworth's intention in a large and carefully constructed work that they must be taken for more than casual indulgence in self-regarding pietism or devotional sweetness.

In his changes to *The Pedlar* Wordsworth does not simply gainsay the past: he refashions it completely. Originally, we have seen, this was a narrative poem in which the Pedlar first told his tale of suffering and then subjected it to a cheerful necessitarian interpretation. These are the final lines of his lengthy argument:

> "My Friend, enough to sorrow have you given,
> The purposes of Wisdom asks no more,
> Be wise and cheerful, and no longer read
> The forms of things with an unworthy eye.
> She sleeps in the calm earth and peace is here.
> I well remember that those very plumes,
> Those weeds and the high spear-grass on that wall,
> By mist and silent rain-drops silvered o'er,
> As once I passed, did to my mind convey
> So still an image of tranquillity,
> So calm and still, and looked so beautiful,
> Amid the uneasy thoughts which filled my mind,
> That what we feel of sorrow and despair
> From ruin and from change, and all the grief
> The passing shews of being leave behind
> Appeared an idle dream that could not live
> Where meditation was. I turned away
> And walked along my road in happiness."
> He ceased. . . .[1]

"Meditation" comes at the end of the long and finely managed sentence that dominates this passage. It is the classical Wordsworthian abstract noun, referred to time and space through association with the verb "to

[1] *P.W.*, Vol. V. p. 403.

be", and so positioned, almost pointed at—"where
meditation was"—as to gain the authority peculiar to
the concrete and the evidence of things seen. It is one
of Wordsworth's Presences, vast and yet precise in
their encompassing of thing and thought. Wordsworth was wise to follow Humpty Dumpty's example
and pay his word extra, for it has a great deal of work
to do, gathering in the fruit of the Pedlar's prolonged
philosophizing. The point of "meditation", in the
Pedlar's own summary of his argument, is that by

> deeply drinking in the soul of things
> We shall be wise perforce, and we shall move
> From strict necessity along the path
> Of order and of good.[1]

And however shoddy the Pedlar's reasoning, there lies
beyond it an entire poetry of joy and natural good.
This is what makes a triumph of his great conclusion.

When it was published, *The Pedlar* became the first
book of *The Excursion*. The story remains in substance
the same, but its moral is profoundly altered; for the
Pedlar's necessitarian argument, designed in the first
place to counter the fact of suffering, is entirely
omitted, and in the final text his conclusion is restated
in Christian terms. Wordsworth's immediate response
to his tale of Margaret's miserable death in the ruined
cottage gives warning of change:

> I blessed her in the impotence of grief.[2]

And although the Pedlar still rebukes him, he does so
for a different reason:

> My Friend! enough to sorrow you have given,
> The purposes of wisdom ask no more:
> Nor more would she have craved as due to One
> Who, in her worst distress, had ofttimes felt
> The unbounded might of prayer; and learned, with soul

[1] *P.W.*, Vol. V. p. 402.   [2] l. 924.

> Fixed on the Cross, that consolation springs,
> From sources deeper far than deepest pain,
> For the meek Sufferer. Why then should we read
> The forms of things with an unworthy eye ?[1]

And so on, as before. But "meditation" has gone, and in its place is the assertion that grief

> Appeared an idle dream, that could maintain,
> Nowhere, dominion o'er the enlightened spirit
> Whose meditative sympathies repose
> Upon the breast of Faith.[2]

In *Peter Bell*, the entry of a concurrent Christian interest simply makes nonsense of the poem's naturalism. *The Pedlar*, on the other hand, still makes sense, but sense quite opposed to Wordsworth's original intention. Certainly it is of no immediate poetic interest that Hartleian philosophy has given way to a Christian statement of the problem of pain, clearly made and without compromise, but still with little imaginative force. We have nevertheless a preliminary advantage in knowing that Wordsworth's deliberate alteration of his poems cannot be dismissed as shamefaced tinkering with work that might displease the orthodox. There is no doubt that he was trying to write Christian poetry, and not merely to appear respectable.

It is also certain that Wordsworth's poetry was not changed by conscious application only, although what was meant and what was not are often hard to distinguish. Even in the 1850 *Prelude*, where his work is singularly deliberate, intentional and unintentional go hand in hand. At the beginning of the last book there is described a night ascent of Snowdon, which was written, like other great passages in the later books, certainly or probably during the marvellous years of 1798 and 1799. Wordsworth says, in the 1805 text of

[1] l. 932.   [2] l. 952.

The Prelude, that the scene from the top of the mountain

>   appear'd to me
> The perfect image of a mighty Mind,
> Of one that feeds upon infinity,
> That is exalted by an underpresence,
> The sense of God, or whatsoe'er is dim
> Or vast in its own being. . . .[1]

Out of its context this reads like muddy bombast, vaguely pantheistic in flavour. But I cannot believe that Wordsworth was much worried about its theological correctness when he altered and expanded it in this way:

> There I beheld the emblem of a mind
> That feeds upon infinity, that broods
> Over the dark abyss, intent to hear
> Its voices issuing forth to silent light
> In one continuous stream; a mind sustained
> By recognitions of transcendent power,
> In sense conducted to ideal form,
> In soul of more than mortal privilege.[2]

Now this is not much clearer than the 1805 account, but the impression that it leaves is utterly different. "Image" has become "emblem"—a significant change in Wordsworth—and everything conspires to set the mind over against the object of its attention. The mind "broods", "intent to hear" voices rising from below; and Wordsworth's picture is then generalized and given intellectual depth by reference to the Platonic vision of "ideal form" transcending the world of sense.

At this point it becomes profitless to talk about Wordsworth's intentions. His state of mind when he made these changes would probably, if it could be discovered, help us not at all. His earlier account felt

[1] Bk. XIII. 68.   [2] 1850, Bk. XIV. 70.

wrong to him: he could no longer say it like that. The mood of cloudy exaltation which it recalled so effectively now embarrassed and perplexed him. This was more what he meant. And so he undertook *The Prelude's* revision, often very unclear what was the matter with it, and unable for the most part to attempt more than fragmentary restatement; but no doubt consoled by the way in which the late *Prelude* of 1804 and 1805 had already worked deep change in the poem's quality, with its doctrine of spiritual love and its final rejoicing in the mind sovereign over nature.

Much more relevant than the question of intention is that of alteration in the imaginative stuff of the Great Decade. I have already mentioned two solitaries who appear in the late *Prelude*.[1] The shepherd

> descried in distant sky,
> A solitary object and sublime,
> Above all height! like an aerial Cross. . . .

exemplifies the mock sublime and Wordsworth's straining for a transcendental poetry, comparable with his feeble defence of old age in *The Excursion*, as a state of complete detachment. The blind beggar in London, wearing a label that was for Wordsworth

> a type,
> Or emblem of the utmost that we know,
> Both of ourselves and of the universe. . . .

I have thought of as relevant to the poetry of indecision. But "emblem" suggests that he may be important in a different way; and this is borne out at the end of the encounter:

> on the shape of the unmoving man,
> His fixèd face and sightless eyes, I look'd
> As if admonish'd from another world.

[1] See pp. 126-8.

The beggar is not a natural Presence, like the early solitaries, but an intimation of otherness. He confirms the change already discernible a year or two before, in the figure of the Leech-Gatherer, who seemed

> like a man from some far region sent,
> To give me human strength, by apt admonishment.

These are signs of revolution in the primary materials of Wordsworth's poetry; and the same can be said of childhood as of solitude. It is upon childhood that Wordsworth bases his idea of solitude-in-relationship in the early *Prelude;* for childhood is the great natural fact which demonstrates the perfect working of "those first-born affinities that fit Our new existence to existing things". But when Wordsworth returns to childhood in Book V, he has developed an interest that extends beyond the natural order. "Our childhood," he says,

> Our simple childhood sits upon a throne
> That hath more power than all the elements.
> I guess not what this tells of Being past,
> Nor what it augurs of the life to come,
> But so it is. . . .[1]

And he goes on to describe childhood as "that dubious hour, that twilight", making his meaning finally clear by calling it an

> isthmus which we cross
> In progress from our native continent
> To earth and human life. . . .[2]

He is beginning to think of childhood as a bridge between God and man.

Book V of *The Prelude* was written in the spring of 1804; and it has been argued, on the strength of internal evidence, that the second part of the Im-

[1] Bk. V. 532.   [2] l. 560.

mortality Ode was written at the same time.[1] Comparison of the passage we have just considered with the opening lines of the fifth stanza suggests to me that this is true:

> Our birth is but a sleep and a forgetting:
> The Soul that rises with us, our life's Star,
>   Hath had elsewhere its setting,
>   And cometh from afar:
>   Not in entire forgetfulness,
>   And not in utter nakedness,
> But trailing clouds of glory do we come
>   From God, who is our home:
> Heaven lies about us in our infancy!

In both cases Wordsworth is regarding childhood in the same way, but the mere sketch of *The Prelude* becomes in the Immortality Ode the pivot of his argument for the undying soul. Childhood is a revelation of "our native continent", or of "God, who is our home"; valued not for its solid and comprehensive hereness, but for its thereness, its power to illuminate the other.

At the outset I stressed Wordsworth's early monism because his late Christianity cannot be understood without it. In so far as he thought seriously about heaven and earth, it was as two aspects of the same thing. Now, in his treatment of solitude and childhood, we see him beginning to think of them as two different things. This is no play with words, with alternative means of expressing one idea: movement of this kind is the profoundest crisis that the life of the mind can suffer. In his own note to the Immortality Ode, Wordsworth defends his use of the doctrine of pre-existence in these words:

> Archimedes said that he could move the world if he had a point whereon to rest his machine. Who has not felt the same aspirations as regards the world of his own mind? Having to

[1] *P.W.*, Vol. IV. pp. 464-5.

wield some of its elements when I was impelled to write this poem on the *Immortality of the Soul*, I took hold of the notion of pre-existence as having sufficient foundation in humanity for authorizing me to make for my purpose the best use of it I could as a poet.[1]

Despite its bland tone, this is an admission of the first importance. Wordsworth had always intended, in entire seriousness, to "move the world" through his poetry; and he had once felt able, by sustained and Spinozistic paradox, to do so from within. But in the Immortality Ode he is preparing himself for the defeat of his imaginative monism: the answer to the world must be outside the world. Coleridge also acknowledged this, and left Spinoza for Christian orthodoxy. But in philosophy he thought his way back into the profounder monism of the German School: hence the tension of his thought and his confused utterance. Wordsworth escaped this dilemma because he was not the man to see the clash of old and new in speculative terms. But his own difficulties were no less real.

This work of 1804 anticipates Wordsworth's response to the death of his brother John which occurred a few months later. Under the immediate stress of pain and bewilderment he asserted an extreme religious dualism: the evils of earthly existence, he said, seemed to him inexplicable "except on the supposition of *another* and a *better world*"[2]; and he thought of his brother as going "to that God from whom I trust he will receive his reward".[3] Later, he consoled Southey in bereavement as he had consoled himself, with the expectation of "another and a more stable world",[4] venturing at another time the generalization that "all religions owe their origin or acceptation to the wish of

[1] *P.W.*, Vol. IV. p. 464.
[2] *Early Letters* (ed. de Selincourt), p. 460.
[3] *Ibid.*, p. 486.
[4] *Letters*, 1811-20 (ed. de Selincourt), p. 736.

the human heart to supply in another state of existence the deficiences of this. . . ."[1]

The most certain thing about Wordsworth's religion is its initial poverty. Little more than an admission of defeat in a long war of which his brother's death was the last and decisive battle, it had at first no chance of engaging his finer powers. It lacked joy and creative interest and, in a sense, conviction, for a man is not entirely convinced of necessity: there is a difference between admitting and accepting the truth. Moreover, Wordsworth's imagination had certain natural limits which it never overstepped. His slender knowledge of sin is primarily responsible for the weak optimism of his late Christian Pastoral: he wanted Coleridge's lively sense of the enemy within, and an entire world of religious experience was thereby closed to him. Nor could he write about Christian doctrine. He had not the intellectual strength for sustained theological argument, nor the agility for metaphysical wit-writing. Wit-writing of every kind had always been foreign to his solemn and literal talent: if he had heard Coleridge declare that the stars appeared to him, one misty night, "like full stops on damp paper",[2] Wordsworth would have been almost shocked.

It is also true that Wordsworth's Christianity often made matters worse, as in *Peter Bell*, by augmenting chaos. I have taken *The White Doe* as the very type of indecision; but *The Excursion* would have done as well, were it not planned on a much larger and less manageable scale. The form of loose dialogue between persons of ill-defined character and opinion is exactly suited to the voicing of personal doubts, and the result is a scrapbook history of Wordsworth's imaginative life. The past is here: praise of solitude that "permits the mind to feel", and of relationship with the natural world in

[1] *Letters*, 1821-30 (ed. de Selincourt), p. 134.
[2] *Anima Poetae* (ed. E. H. Coleridge), p. 45.

which the "mind gives back the various forms of things". There is rejoicing in the visionary innocence of childhood, and lamentation over its departure following "sad exclusion from decay of sense". The Pedlar's Hartleian philosophy of long ago is now transferred to the fourth book, where it rubs shoulders with an invocation of the state in which

> the mind admits
> The law of duty; and can therefore move
> Through each vicissitude of loss and gain,
> Linked in entire complacence with her choice.[1]

One character asserts that the only "adequate support For the calamities of mortal life" is "an assured belief" in "a Being Of infinite benevolence and power"; and then, fifty lines later in the same discourse, he asks himself, "what are things eternal?", and answers:

> subject neither to eclipse nor wane,
> Duty exists;—immutably survive,
> For our support, the measures and the forms,
> Which an abstract intelligence supplies. . . .[2]

And there is much transcendental yearning after "that pure and unknown world of love Where injury cannot come". *The Excursion* suffers for its large design. Wordsworth devoted so much of his middle age to it that it could not fail to commemorate the period of flux, and often it gets the worst of all worlds. He felt himself that the poem was inconclusive as he had finished it, for he intended to continue the story with an account of the sceptical Solitary witnessing "some religious ceremony—a sacrament, say, in the open fields, or a preaching among the mountains",[3] and this was to have "done more towards restoring the Christian faith in which he had been educated, and, with that, contentedness and even cheerfulness of mind,

---

[1] Bk. IV. 1035.   [2] *Ibid.*, 72.   [3] *P.W.*, Vol. V. p. 474.

than all that the Wanderer and Pastor, by their several
effusions and addresses, had been able to effect. An
issue like this was in my intentions". All this sounds
ominous enough: religious-pastoral is one of the most
tedious of his late manners. But at the same time it
reveals an uncertainty of purpose too profound to be
entirely conscious.

What is new and Christian in *The Excursion* is not
always ineffectual. Wordsworth can still write per-
suasively of things that he has seen, though his gaze
is now heavenward:

> homeward the shepherds moved
> Through the dull mist, I following—when a step,
> A single step that freed me from the skirts
> Of the blind vapour, opened to my view
> Glory beyond all glory ever seen
> By waking sense or by the dreaming soul!
> The appearance, instantaneously disclosed,
> Was of a mighty city—boldly say
> A wilderness of building, sinking far
> And self-withdrawn into a boundless depth,
> Far sinking into splendour—without end!
> Fabric it seemed of diamond and of gold,
> With alabaster domes, and silver spires,
> And blazing terrace upon terrace. . . .[1]

And while his eyes are raised to the Kingdom of
Heaven, he still stands on earth; so that there is fugue-
like movement of finite and infinite through the
passage. The immediate occasion of the experience is
clearly stated:

> By earthly nature had the effect been wrought
> Upon the dark materials of the storm
> Now pacified. . . .

[1] Bk. II. 828.

But no less clear, as he returns to it, is the sight of

> that marvellous array
> Of temple, palace, citadel, and huge
> Fantastic pomp of structure without name. . . .

Finally, the contrast of familiar valley and city that has suddenly usurped it, becomes explicit:

> This little Vale, a dwelling-place of Man,
> Lay low beneath my feet; 'twas visible—
> I saw not, but I felt that it was there.
> That which I *saw* was the revealed abode
> Of Spirits in beatitude. . . .
>   . . . there I stood and gazed:
> The apparition faded not away,
> And I descended.

Wordsworth sees Paradise as a jewelled and holy city, as the New Jerusalem of Revelation. That the city should play this part is at once remarkable, since it has hitherto been very unimportant to him. The city of social and satirical poetry appears scarcely at all, because he was not this kind of poet. The city has no place within the greater landscape: if it has any poetic function, it is the negative one of circumscribing the unmanageable. This is not to say that all Wordsworth's poetry of the city is bad: sometimes, as in *The Prelude's* description of the "anarchy and din" of St Bartholomew's Fair, the countryman's wide-eyed stare, his fearful amazement, his almost unwilling fascination, are vividly conveyed. And once or twice, as when he saw London from Westminster Bridge "all bright and glittering" in the dress of early morning, or, in a fine poem which he left unpublished,

> white with winter's purest white, as fair,
> As fresh and spotless as he ever sheds
> On field or mountain,[1]

[1] *P.W.*, Vol. IV. p. 374.

the city is suddenly transmuted, and one can just understand how he came to see that other that has no need
of sun or moon to shine upon it.

Even so, the *Excursion* city is a new thing—Paradise in an exact Christian and literary sense. It would be
a tidy thesis that followed Wordsworth's imaginative
course from the Garden of Eden in his greater landscape to the New Jerusalem in his late poetry. But it
would not be true. The landscape is paradisal only in
that difficult sense in which Wordsworth's early poetry
is optimistic. Neither is it Christian nor is it the Never
Never Land of Classical and Rousseauite myth: it is
northern and severe, with a terrible simplicity that the
pastoral Wordsworth of Arnold's tradition could not
have compassed. And Wordsworth did not see his landscape as he now sees the holy city. Then, the point of
his vision was the literalness that enabled him, as he
insisted in a hundred different ways, to see things as
they are. Now there is a duality which he openly admits.
The valley "was visible", yet he did not see it. What he
saw—and he italicizes the word so that there shall be
no mistake—was "the revealed abode" of the blessed.
"Revealed" emphasizes the divine gift of second-
sight. We must believe that Wordsworth was in the
spirit when he beheld this vision.

Nor does Wordsworth's spiritual eye report anything grey or ghostly: the picture is as brilliant and as
substantial as that described in Revelation. This directness of visual appeal owes much to the philosophical
innocence that allowed Wordsworth to write about the
Kingdom of Heaven unalarmed by the huge difficulties
at least as old as Plato's *Parmenides*, that attend belief
in a transcendent order of reality. In this *Excursion*
passage he is entirely concerned, like Blake, to report
what he saw, in the faith that visions justify themselves;
and, like Blake, he sees his problem as one of adequate
description. Sustained prophetic frenzy is very rare in

Wordsworth, but he is clearly attracted to the lunatic state, as to childhood, for its privileged access to the supernatural. A late poem about a woman driven mad by the pain of bereavement ends thus:

Nor of those maniacs is she one that kiss
The air or laugh upon a precipice;
No, passing through strange sufferings towards the tomb,
She smiles as if a martyr's crown were won:
Oft, when light breaks through clouds or waving trees,
With outspread arms and fallen upon her knees
The Mother hails in her descending Son
An Angel, and in earthly ecstacies
Her own angelic glory seems begun.[1]

The Christianity of this poetry is very unlike that which inspired the almost incredible final couplet of his *Address to a Skylark:*

I, with my fate contented, will plod on,
And hope for higher raptures, when life's day is done.

Anything but mean and pinched, its nature is already being unfolded in the architecture and jewelry of the holy city, and in the ceremonious action of lunacy— demoniac with those that "laugh upon a precipice" and adoring with the woman "fallen upon her knees": for art and symbolic action and eternity precious and unbreathing are the subject of his late poetry.

The Immortality Ode once more proves a turning-point. Arnold, and many since Arnold, have been offended by what they take for an unwordsworthian element in the ode's imagery and diction. The child comes earthward from an "imperial palace". The lambs that "bound As to the tabor's sound" discover the rhythm of their game in the Old Testament. The ode is suggestive of ritual form in "jubilee", "festival", "wedding", "funeral"; in "my head hath its coronal",

---

[1] *The Widow on Windermere Side.*

in "the gladness of the May", in "other palms are won". Critics are right to complain, but wrong to take no further interest in these discordancies.

The same thing happens in *The Prelude*, and is partly responsible for the discreteness of the later version.

> Witness, ye Solitudes! where I received
> My earliest visitations[1]

in the 1805 text becomes in 1850

> compassed round by mountain solitudes,
> Within whose solemn temple I received
> My earliest visitations. . . .[2]

Wordsworth is not simply indulging his taste for circumlocution. The God-graven temple of earth is one of the most persistent images in his late poetry, and one aspect of his changed attitude to the entire natural order. The idea of God as mere Creator is still repugnant to him: he follows his own advice, which was, we have seen, to "say as little as possible about *making*".[3] But God the loving and careful Artist—Wordsworth's theory of art, unlike Coleridge's, was not a theory of making—and God the Sustainer are both familiar.

Again, in the 1805 *Prelude*, he speaks of men of great soul who, in their dealings "with all the objects of the universe",

> for themselves create
> A like existence; and, whene'er it is
> Created for them, catch it by an instinct.[4]

In 1850, "all the objects" becomes "the whole compass", indicative of Wordsworth's loss of concentration upon particularity and the reciprocal principle; and the rest is much altered:

---

[1] Bk. XIII. 123.   [2] Bk. XIV. 139.
[3] Page 36.   [4] Bk. XIII. 94.

> for themselves create
> A like existence; and whene'er it dawns
> Created for them, catch it, or are caught
> By its inevitable mastery,
> Like angels stopped upon the wing by sound
> Of harmony from Heaven's remotest spheres.[1]

Clearly Wordsworth has come to dislike "instinct", with its natural and optimistic associations. In its place he introduces the equivocal "catch it, or are caught", and adds to this the angel simile. The simile is worth attention: it is more than a Miltonic flourish, just as the retreat from instinct is not mere cowardice or dishonesty. Wordsworth's movement from nature is also a movement towards art. There is an ever-increasing emphasis upon craftsmanship in his talk about poetry, and in his practice there is more of literary. Because of this, criticism that fails to use the criterion of Derivative with great tact may well go astray. Thus in the present case, the obvious Miltonism of the last line must not hide the sudden arrest of "angels stopped upon the wing", which is very effective and not quite Miltonic. And as for the general, angels work hard and successfully in Wordsworth's late poetry, speaking of heaven and earth as he requires them.

Angels live in heaven, but are sometimes seen by men. Thus they are persuaded by the beauty of spring on earth to "quit their mansions unsusceptible of change"[2] and walk abroad. Or a merciful errand may bring them here: Wordsworth tells how

> their own untroubled home
> They leave, and speed on nightly embassy
> To visit earthly chambers.[3]

They may have a purpose less specific than this comforting of sufferers. When attention seems wholly

---

[1] Bk. XIV. 94.   [2] *Vernal Ode.*   [3] *The Cuckoo Clock.*

directed towards earth they sometimes remind us un-
expectedly of the other order:

> In sunny glade,
> Or under leaves of thickest shade,
> Was such a stillness e'er diffused
> Since earth grew calm while angels mused ?[1]

This extreme delicacy with firmness of suggestion is
the angelic task. Their transcendentalism is often, as
here, a matter of being convincingly apart; or, like the
child, of coming from the courts of the holy city. And
they have their natural counterparts, in Wordsworth's
late poetry, in the heavenly bodies: in the moon,
looking down upon the earth's "unsettled atmos-
phere",[2] in order to "shield from harm the humblest
of the sleeping"; and the sun, "source inexhaustible
of life and joy", worshipped once as "a blazing intellectual deity".[3] *The Excursion* opens with the prayer
that the poem may shine "star-like", secure from
"those mutations that extend their sway Throughout
the nether sphere"[4]; and it closes[5] with the analogy,
too carefully developed, of the sun and the Deity. The
invisible sun, shedding light on evening clouds, is
called "this local transitory type Of thy paternal splen-
dours". And when Wordsworth hears the cuckoo, his
favourite among sky creatures,

> Wandering in solitude, and evermore
> Foretelling and proclaiming,[6]

---

[1] *The Triad.*
[2] *To the Moon.*
[3] *To the Clouds.*
[4] The very sharp contrast of Star-Poem and "nether sphere" only
appears in later versions of the Preface. In his first draft Wordsworth
merely expresses the hope
> that my song may live, and be
> Even as a light hung up in heaven to cheer
> The world in times to come.   (*P.W.*, Vol. V. p. 6).
[5] Bk. IX. 590-633.
[6] *The Cuckoo at Laverna.*

he is now put in mind of

> the great Prophet, styled *the Voice of One*
> *Crying amid the wilderness.*

Everything in nature speaks of its Original to one who
listens

> in the power, the faith,
> Of a baptized imagination.

Angels and shining things of earth serve Wordsworth's purpose in another way. Consider this glance
at the world through a magnifying glass:

> Glasses he had, that little things display,
> The beetle panoplied in gems and gold,
> A mailéd angel on a battle-day;
> The mysteries that cups of flowers enfold. . . .[1]

Unnatural in the way of art in its jewelled proportion,
the universe becomes a bright pageant that relates to
God with a fineness too elusive for the wide-meshed
vocabulary of symbol and analogy. Mastery of scale, in
the shift from beetle to angelic wars, is another aspect
of Wordsworth's understanding of God the Artist; and
later, in the great *Vernal Ode*, he exploits it to marvellous effect. He is resting his "tired lute", after a song
of time and immortality, when there steals upon his ear

> the soft murmur of the vagrant Bee.
> —A slender sound! Yet hoary Time
> Doth to the *Soul* exalt it with the chime
> Of all his years;—a company
> Of ages coming, ages gone;
> (Nations from before them sweeping,
> Regions in destruction steeping,)
> But every awful sound in unison
> With that faint utterance, which tells
> Of treasure sucked from buds and bells,
> For the pure keeping of those waxen cells.

[1] *Within our happy Castle* . . .

Then Wordsworth describes her pausing in flight, so
that he can observe her parts:

> o'er this tempting flower
> Hovering, until the petals stay
> Her flight, and take its voice away!—
> Observe each wing!—a tiny van!
> The structure of her laden thigh,
> How fragile! yet of ancestry
> Mysteriously remote and high;
> High as the imperial front of man;
> The roseate bloom on woman's cheek;
> The soaring eagle's curvèd beak;
> The white plumes of the floating swan;
> Old as the tiger's paw. . . .

Scale is important for this reason, that by beating the
bounds of creation, from the nature of time to the bee's
humming and from her wing and thigh to tiger's paw,
Wordsworth is able to suggest how God must see his
own work. There is artistic love and justice in the
handling of each element, none preferred before the
rest since there is no small and no great within the work
of art, but mutual support towards the end of coherence
and beauty. Everything is intelligible in terms of everything else, as, by divine transposition, the temporal
order in the voice of the bee; and the whole leans on the
Artist's imaginative will. The idea of service directed
to God's glory replaces the self-sustaining structure of
the greater landscape: in terse little poems, not unlike
those of Yeats's old age, Wordsworth sees the shadow
of a daisy fulfil its nature by protecting a dew-drop
from the sun,[1] or moon and planet together in the sky
and wonders which is queen and which attendant.[2]
In natural things there is a new bright meaning:
beak and plume and paw are the elements of a living

[1] *To a Child, Written in her Album.*
[2] *The Crescent-moon.*

heraldry, closely related to Wordsworth's jewelry and architecture, and adding to these the more urgent quality of ceremonious action. Only a poet grown old in wisdom would dare to use the conventions of "hoary time", "imperial front", "roseate bloom", because they exactly serve his purpose. The utterly conventional can thus approach the command of style proper to divinity.

Another aspect of heraldic nature is its anthropomorphism, mythical and heroic. Wordsworth at one time protested against the use of Classical mythology, as a kind of decadence. In a sonnet to a brook he said:

> If wish were mine some type of thee to view,
> Thee, and not thee thyself, I would not do
> Like Grecian Artists, give thee human cheeks,
> Channels for tears; no Naiad shouldst thou be. . . .[1]

The root of his objection is the offence that this sort of thing gives to his philosophy of inner and outer, the independence of each and the "ennobling interchange" between them. Nor in truth did he recant, for his late poetry is not in this sense anthropomorphic. Natural objects are not men in disguise; but there is a certain key, reached again through a kind of divine transposition, in which human inference may be drawn from all the music of the world. He speaks of trees that "tear The lingering remnant of their yellow hair",[2] of the eagle "shedding where he flew Loose fragments of wild wailing",[3] of waterfalls "white-robed"[4]— priestlike, perhaps, as Keats's "moving waters". The only Roman among the English Romantics, Wordsworth still went to Greece for his mythology, and he made of it something strong and personal. Because

---

[1] *Brook! whose society . . .*
[2] *One who was suffering tumult . . .*
[3] *A dark plume fetch me . . .*
[4] *The Excursion*, Bk. III. 48.

things are seen in God's eye, the anthropomorphism of nature is curiously without human prejudice or condescension.

The same bee of the *Vernal Ode* is called

a warrior bold,
κadiant all over with unburnished gold,
And armed with living spear for mortal fight;
A cunning forager
That spreads no waste, a social builder; one
In whom all busy offices unite
With all fine functions that afford delight.

In his *Georgics*, Vergil compares bees to men, and later, in *The Æneid*, men to bees: a coming full circle that has been related to his poetry's development.[1] Wordsworth is doing neither—or both. Warrior, forager, social builder are impartial titles, above and between the bee-world and the man-world, which have both an equal claim to them. And again the angelic brightness of description marks a divine authenticity, the impress of the Just Artist's hands on all his creatures. Art in this way becomes the heart of Wordsworth's late poetry, and figures like the humming-bee its agents. Through the bee's embracing of all functions, warlike, peaceful, utilitarian, ornamental, art achieves the controlled boundlessness proper to itself. If the bee-world can be described in terms intelligible to men, but without reducing bees to men in miniature, we will know better how God sees us, and what it is like to be concerned in heaven for happenings on earth. Art helps in this because of its power to lay paradox to rest: it is at once the hardest work and the purest play; it matters finally and finally it does not matter, since love which is richness of art is not quite love which is richness of life— yet it is still love, and godlike in the artist's simultaneous detachment and participation; so that heat and

[1] W. F. J. Knight, *Roman Vergil*, pp. 167, 170.

light are undiminished, and he can escape, though only in imagination, the precise human self-involvement that makes divine compassion unattainable.

The flowers of Wordsworth's poetry are no longer studied with literal passion, to discover what they are. Already, in the Immortality Ode, the "pansy at my feet" is completely formal, introduced with the barest of gestures to confirm Wordsworth's story of lost childhood, and interesting only for its relevance to the human predicament. Flowers, like the *Vernal Ode* bee, supply a transcendental correlative for the root situations of men. "The flowers themselves," with

> all their glistening,
> Call to the heart for inward listening—
> And though for bridal wreaths and tokens true
> Welcomed wisely; though a growth
> Which the careless shepherd sleeps on,
> As fitly spring from turf the mourner weeps on—
> And without wrong are cropped the marble tomb to strew.[1]

Again there is convention and ceremony, and the comprehension at remove peculiar to art.

In a very late poem, *Love Lies Bleeding*, the same elements are present, and their organization is most subtle. Wordsworth's theme is the red flower that is always drooping, seems always to be dying, yet never dies, its "life passing not away":

> A flower how rich in sadness! Even thus stoops,
> (Sentient by Grecian sculpture's marvellous power),
> Thus leans, with hanging brow and body bent
> Earthward in uncomplaining languishment,
> The dying Gladiator. So, sad Flower!
> ('Tis Fancy guides me willing to be led,
> Though by a slender thread,)
> So drooped Adonis, bathed in sanguine dew
> Of his death-wound, when he from innocent air

[1] *The Triad.*

The gentlest breath of resignation drew;
While Venus in a passion of despair
Rent, weeping over him, her golden hair
Spangled with drops of that celestial shower.
She suffered, as Immortals sometimes do. . . .

The flower is compared with the sculptured figure that
seems to be alive, and then with the mythical—the
fighter and the lover who were both killed in sport.
This is a large achievement in very small compass;
ranging from flesh to stone and from stone to story,
learning from each the same lesson which is also
different because of their varying conditions. The
passage has a great and almost anonymous distinction,
like the blue of sky, and seems to resolve the inexplicable
in its subject through some mystery of style. Wordsworth the unfanciful has reached an extreme of fancy
which before and since has been the province of old
imaginations.

This preoccupation with mere art is seen to be
nothing limited. The starlit dome, in Yeats's *Byzantium*,

disdains
All that man is,
All mere complexities,
The fury and the mire of human veins.

Wordsworth also moves towards art, but not in order
to oppose it to nature as Yeats does. His art is not in
this way disdainful: there is no parallel to Yeats's
rhetorical ascent towards his "artifice of eternity".
Wordsworth placed the same human limits on art as on
nature, but the difference between the two orders, as he
experienced it, helped him in his poetry. *Love Lies
Bleeding* has an added richness in its expression of
suffering through art. All the figures suffer, in the
modes of statuesque, literary and pictorial; until in the
end suffering and immortality are brought together.

It was the fact of suffering that first set Wordsworth thinking about the necessity of "another and a better world": struck down by his brother's death, he suggested an answer which may easily prove small and rigid; a philosophy of pain, of life to be undergone but not assented to. That he escaped such an issue is due to his taking firm hold of the fact that God too must suffer. We have already studied *Hart-Leap Well* as an essay in the problem of pain, in which Wordsworth is undecided whether he is writing a landscape poem about an animal that dies where it was born, or asserting God's love for "unoffending creatures" like the hart.[1] There is a third possibility, not hinted at in the poem, but clearly in Wordsworth's mind when he wrote some blank-verse lines a very short time before *Hart-Leap Well* itself. He says that a trance came over him when he stood at the well, thinking about the

> hunted beast, who there
> Had yielded up his breath, the awful trance,
> The vision of humanity, and of God
> The Mourner, God the Sufferer, when the heart
> Of his poor Creatures suffers wrongfully. . . .[2]

Hart-Leap Well was written too soon for Wordsworth to turn this experience to account. Later, in *Love Lies Bleeding* and in other poems, he is able to think of sadness as a kind of wealth, and suffering not without its divine likeness. And Wordsworth's Christianity also becomes rich, through acceptance of the consequences of the Incarnation. Eternal movement from heaven earthward, there manifested, justifies poetic effort; for although the poet must nourish his imagination at the "secondary founts" of time and space, he is still being "tutored for eternity".

In this there is a leaning on God, in His guarantee of the world for poets as for all men. Wordsworth

---

[1] Pages 138-40.   [2] *P.W.*, Vol. V. p. 319.

N

accepts Bradley's dramatic conclusion that appearance *is* reality, but the conclusion rests in the life of the Trinity, as a matter of faith. In his early poetry the star is an important feature of the greater landscape: it helps the Pedlar, in his childhood, to reach thought-in-sense, and is one of the types of eternity. Now it serves a general transcendental purpose, and is of particular interest for its power "to testify of Love and Grace divine". The stars appear

> to mortal eye,
> Blended in absolute serenity,
> And free from semblance of decline;[1]

and the certain mortality of stars does not gainsay this appearance:

> What if those bright fires
> Shine subject to decay,
> Sons haply of extinguished sires,
> Themselves to lose their light, or pass away
> Like clouds before the wind,
> Be thanks poured out to Him whose hand bestows,
> Nightly, on human kind
> That vision of endurance and repose.

Often, as here in the *Vernal Ode*, reliance on the hand that sustains through mortal change and gratitude to the hand that bestows, are found together. In *The Primrose of the Rock*, Wordsworth thinks of the flower as a "link in Nature's chain", and traces this chain, link by link, to God. His late lyrical verse, Christian and conventional rather in the manner of eighteenth-century hymns, has been underestimated by those anxious to see this much and to see no more. Originality has many kinds: Wordsworth, like Burke, his counsellor in politics, can handle received ideas with authority deriving from a serene largeness of scale and vital

---

[1] *Vernal Ode.*

control of emphasis. This primrose he sees, in its
stem

> faithful to the root,
> That worketh out of view;
> And to the rock the root adheres
> In every fibre true.
>
> Close clings to earth the living rock,
> Though threatening still to fall;
> The earth is constant to her sphere;
> And God upholds them all:
> So blooms this lonely Plant, nor dreads
> Her annual funeral.

The immortality of succession becomes very dear to
Wordsworth, as an earthly witness of eternal creative
purpose. It also helps him in his personal struggle for
humility and abatement of natural egotism: he is always
trying to see himself a creature, to impress his finitude.
In 1845 he instructed his printer to place a short
passage of blank verse at the beginning of the volume,
because, he said, "I mean it to serve as a sort of Preface".[1] This is not a good poem, but it catches this
particular quality of his old age. He is once more
watching the night sky, and the stars, some brilliant
others dim, all owing their light to God. And he
addresses himself thus:

> Then, to the measure of the light vouchsafed,
> Shine, Poet! in thy place, and be content.

His putting himself in his place has important consequences. Humility issues into thanks to God for all
good things, and especially for the beauty of nature.
Again perfectly conventional, his attitude is still worth
consideration. What he calls "the religion of gratitude"
can be seen at work in his poetry: gratitude is at the
centre of his religious life because, as he declares,

[1] *P.W.*, Vol. I. p. 317.

"gratitude is the handmaid to hope, and hope the har-
binger of faith".[1] It is as if he returned in different
spirit to his first belief in the necessary connexion of
poetry and pleasure. Pleasure that is coloured by gratitude to the giver is a sacrificial thing: the very taking
joy becomes a handing back to God. As the motto of
his Ecclesiastical Sonnets Wordsworth uses an adaptation of George Herbert's couplet:

> A verse may finde him, who a sermon flies
> And turn delight into a sacrifice:[2]

which makes the point entirely clear; and like other
borrowings in thought and language, it shows how
subtle is the question of originality.

Wordsworth's youth must not be set in judgment
over his old age: nor, of course, must it be denied, as
Wordsworth did when he pretended that he wrote the
Preface to the *Lyrical Ballads* because "prevailed upon
by Mr Coleridge".[3] When he was a young man he felt
impelled to attack the accepted canons of poetic orthodoxy. When he was old, he became orthodox himself.
Both states deserve serious regard; yet there is general
willingness to forgive his youth ignorant and dog-
matic theorising and much bad poetry, while age is
scarcely listened to. Wordsworth found, as an honest
man must, that orthodoxy is no easier than its opposite;
and he could not achieve it without a partial recanta-
tion. In particular, there is his changed attitude to the
conventional in diction and imagery, which at his best
he makes the controlled means of serving new ends. But
this change is itself enough to deny his poetry a hearing:
the eye lights on "hoary time" and "roseate bloom" in
the *Vernal Ode*, and a great poem goes unread.

Convention is thus on the circumference and at the
centre of Wordsworth's late poetry: convention that is

[1] *Letters*, 1821-30 (ed. de Selincourt), p. 204.   [2] *The Church-porch.*
[3] *Letters*, 1831-40 (ed. de Selincourt), p. 910

a plain matter of style leads to convention less plain and already approached through God's artistic manner, through the heraldry of nature and through action determined by accustomed forms—still a matter of style, or concern with the How of things. The last of these, style in ceremony, takes him furthest in his Christian poetry: indeed it proves to be almost the whole truth, since the religion of gratitude makes the imagination everywhere ceremonious, intent to cast experience into a form acceptable to God.

Small wonder, then, that Wordsworth has a lot to say about the ritual of belief. He likes to compare the incense that "curls in clouds Around angelic Forms" depicted on cathedral roof with the "flower-incense" of the fields and "unwearied canticles" of birds and streams.[1] In a more exact sense he is fascinated by the externals of worship. *Processions* is a study of Pagan and Christian within these terms. He recounts how

> mid the sacred grove
> Fed in the Libyan waste by gushing wells,
> The priests and damsels of Ammonian Jove
> Provoked responses with shrill canticles;
> While, in a ship begirt with silver bells,
> They round his altar bore the hornèd God,
> Old Cham, the solar Deity, who dwells
> Aloft, yet in a tilting vessel rode,
> When universal sea the mountains overflowed.

He then turns to "Roman Pomps":

> The feast of Neptune—and the Cereal Games,
> With images, and crowns, and empty cars;
> The dancing Salii—on the shields of Mars
> Smiting with fury; and a deeper dread
> Scattered on all sides by the hideous jars
> Of Corybantian cymbals, while the head
> Of Cybele was seen, sublimely turreted.

[1] *Devotional Incitements.*

And finally to "Christian pageantries": to

> The Cross, in calm procession, borne aloft
> Moved to the chant of sober litanies,

and his sight, one Sunday morning, cf Swiss worshippers

> winding, between Alpine trees
> Spiry and dark, around their House of prayer.

This again is a small poem, but powerful in its dealing with ritual forms. Of all stylistic patterns, Wordsworth sees that of ritual as the most vital and comprehensive: within it he can blend sight and sound and movement in transcendental dedication. It is the favourite retreat of the baptized imagination; and while it serves perfectly the wish to touch all spiritual conditions, it can do so without the narrowness of judgment that seems unavoidable in any direct comparison of creeds. Thus in *Processions* the frenzy and compulsion of pagan rites are justly stated, but without prejudice to the poet's Christianity.

The finest achievement in this kind is the ode *On the Power of Sound*; and not in this kind only, for all the materials of his late poetry are here blended with supreme felicity. As physical eyesight failed, Wordsworth read few books, and he must have seen less as he walked abroad; but he still composed aloud, murmuring by the hour verses to himself. This too, I think, brought him to art in his old age, and a new love for the words themselves: unashamed delight in rhetorical utterance and much experimenting with the regular and the Pindaric ode, its fittest vehicles. Praise of sound, in the present poem, is also homage to poetry, as the thing that he was born to do.

Wordsworth approaches his subject, which is the divinity of sound, by way of the familiar road from nature to art. The voices of all natural things, streams and living creatures; echoes of voice

From rocky steep and rock-bestudded meadows
Flung back, and, in the sky's blue caves, reborn:

the voice that furthers action:

the peasant's whistling breath that lightens
His duteous toil of furrowing the green earth;

the voice that sustains patriot and martyr; the voice
that renders the lunatic

aghast, as at the world
Of reason partially let in—

all lead him to the conclusion stated at the exact middle
of the poem:

Point not these mysteries to an Art
Lodged above the starry pole. . . ?

In its second half the ode enquires more closely how
sound can be art, or "tutored passion". Working with
his favourite elements of story and ritual, Wordsworth
achieves an astonishing result:

The Gift to king Amphion
That walled a city with its melody
Was for belief no dream:—thy skill, Arion!
Could humanize the creatures of the sea,
Where men were monsters. A last grace he craves,
Leave for one chant;—the dulcet sound
Steals from the deck o'er willing waves,
And listening dolphins gather round.
Self-cast, as with a desperate course,
'Mid that strange audience, he bestrides
A proud One docile as a managed horse;
And singing, while the accordant hand
Sweeps his harp, the Master rides;
So shall he touch at length a friendly strand,
And he, with his preserver, shine starbright
In memory, through silent night.

The next stanza opens in heightened and frantic splendour:

> The pipe of Pan, to shepherds
> Couched in the shadow of Maenalian pines,
> Was passing sweet; the eyeballs of the leopards,
> That in high triumph drew the Lord of vines,
> How did they sparkle to the cymbal's clang!
> While Fauns and Satyrs beat the ground
> In cadence,—and Silenus swang
> This way and that, with wild-flowers crowned.

Myth, the kingship of story, a city walled with music; salvation in knowing what song to sing, and bright eternity reached through artistic action—the tale is of some great skill truly learnt, spiritual and gracious like the poetry itself, before it shifts to the terrible brilliance of the leopards' eyeballs and the beating on the ground.

Suddenly Wordsworth returns to the natural order, addressing those "who are longing to be rid Of fable", and bidding them

> hear
> The little sprinkling of cold earth that fell
> Echoed from the coffin-lid.

He then asks why Nature cannot achieve the artistic modulation of her own voices, adding, as a premonition of the truth, this fine Pythagorean comment:

> By one pervading spirit
> Of tones and numbers all things are controlled,
> As sages taught, where faith was found to merit
> Initiation in that mystery old.
> The heavens, whose aspect makes our minds as still
> As they themselves appear to be,
> Innumerable voices fill
> With everlasting harmony;
> The towering headlands, crowned with mist,
> Their feet among the billows, know
> That Ocean is a mighty harmonist. . . .

The Greek answer has already been anticipated by

> What more changeful than the sea?
> But over his great tides
> Fidelity presides,

from another of the late odes.[1] It prepares Wordsworth for his own conclusion. There is a kind of artistry, a meaningful ordering, in nature; in the ebb and flow of air and wash of sea. He had said so long ago, in the poetry of solitude and relationship, building thereon a magnificent and single structure. Glory is not now vanished, nor the affirmative, enfolding optimism of creative purpose: rather, delight becomes a sacrifice, and all this sounding movement confessional of the religion of gratitude:

> All worlds, all natures, mood and measure keep
> For praise and ceaseless gratulation, poured
> Into the ear of God, their Lord!

And so to the final stanza, telling how sound was before the beginning, and will survive the end:

> A Voice to Light gave Being;
> To Time, and Man his earth-born chronicler;
> A Voice shall finish doubt and dim foreseeing,
> And sweep away life's visionary stir;
> The trumpet (we, intoxicate with pride,
> Arm at its blast for deadly wars)
> To archangelic lips applied,
> The grave shall open, quench the stars.

Not sound exactly, but a Voice, which is also, in the poem's final line, "the WORD that shall not pass away". He is using a Semitic and European highroad in this language of the Word, a convention that becomes commandingly personal in his apocalyptic vision of Thought Self-Voiced, of divine Action-in-Utterance

---

[1] *The Triad.*

perfecting the Christian mystery of life. What can be understood by the Word that was made flesh? For this essay the answer must rest in the energy and coherence of Wordsworth's transcendental symbolism.

I would not claim too much. There is no *Tempest* lying unregarded in this late work, or even such poetry as would reverse the universal judgment that the best is early. Even so, it has been grossly underestimated, too easily slipped into place to serve large theories of Romantic defeat. The final privacy of greatness in style has escaped notice. Wordsworth was not silenced by the music of Christianity, nor stifled by Victorian morals. He was profoundly changed. He writes now of stories and strange ritual acts, of "doubt and dim fore-seeing", of the witness of faith and the spiritual eye: his waterfall-trumpeter is now the archangel.

V

EPILOGUE

THERE is an anxious problem of form in treating the work of sixty years within reasonable compass. The outline of a thesis must be clear—otherwise confusion and certain boredom; but it can scarcely be kept so without falling into the false simplicity of caricature: so that I ask help of all kinds, and especially belief in my questions. When, in his later poetry, Wordsworth tells of a noble shepherd, that

> both the undying fish that swim
> Through Bowscale-tarn did wait on him;
> The pair were servants of his eye
> In their immortality;[1]

and of men who

> in bells of crystal dive—
> Where winds and waters cease to strive—
> For no unholy visitings,
> Among the monsters of the Deep;
> And all the sad and precious things
> Which there in ghastly silence sleep;[2]

and of boulders strewn about a deserted mountain pass that appear

> Tents of a camp that never shall be raised:[3]

he is describing the natural world in a way that seems to me at once arresting and utterly foreign to his youth. This raises the largest of my initial questions—one that can be of no interest to him who thinks this verse

---

[1] *Song at the Feast of Brougham Castle.*   [2] *To Enterprise.*
[3] *The Pass of Kirkstone.*

undistinguished, or else close in imagination to Wordsworth's early work.

But if so much is granted, it becomes possible to
walk more delicately. Solitude and childhood, once at
the heart of his early poetry, do not entirely disappear:
they play a different and smaller part, as agents of
otherness; and between this beginning and this end
lies the poetry of indecision. Consider *The Solitary
Reaper*, written in 1805, the year of his brother's death,
of *The Prelude's* conclusion, and of the poem about
Peele Castle; and inviting comparison with Lucy and
the Danish Boy, solitary singers of 1798 and 1799.
The later poem is very successful; but in its quality of
life size, in the precise humanity of its wistfulness—
"Will no one tell me what she sings?"—the singer and
her song are far removed from these others. Again it
seems pertinent to wonder why; to consider where his
middle age is weak, and where, within the limits of a
smaller naturalism, it achieves a certain strength.

Such questions, even if well directed, do not establish universal criteria for literary judgment: they are
personal to Wordsworth, and they serve other ends than
that of judgment, which is but one aspect of the critical
activity and which appears to good effect only when it
attends the struggle to participate. Where I cannot
share I feel most ill at ease. Thus I have been able to
make almost nothing of Wordsworth's heroic manner,
of the careful Miltonic sonnets and the patriotic odes;
and am afraid not of simple blundering as to their
merit, but of a deep failure of apprehension as to their
bearing upon his mind's quality: for there can be no
doubt that an element of the extrovert and brazen runs
through its whole fabric, and works in hidden ways.
The famous sonnets read like exercises, repellent often
in their provincial self-importance and bourgeois noble
enthusiasm. Wordsworth's use of the sonnet, as verse-
paragraph, best shown in the River Duddon Sequence,

is a different matter: here the movement of his meaning
is so attempered to the limits of the medium as to give
a redeeming fluency to his slightest work, as to this,
published in a newspaper and not considered by the
poet to be worth reprinting:

> I find it written of Simonides
> That travelling in strange countries once he found
> A corpse that lay expos'd upon the ground,
> For which, with pains, he caused due obsequies
> To be performed, and paid all holy fees.
> Soon after, this man's Ghost unto him came
> And told him not to sail as was his aim,
> On board a ship then ready for the seas.
> Simonides, admonished by the ghost,
> Remained behind: the ship the following day
> Set sail, was wrecked, and all on board were lost.
> Thus was the tenderest Poet that could be,
> Who sang in ancient Greece his moving lay,
> Saved out of many by his piety.[1]

But his sonnets in the grand manner obtrude their box-
like form until I tire of witnessing so many storms in
so many teacups, and find comfort in the slender story
of Simonides. Even so, it is not enough to dislike this
poetry and to give a reason: I am still uncertain how to
fit it into my picture or how honestly to exclude it—
aware of being defeated by the individuality of consciousness, and not at all sure what it was to be Wordsworth.

Like all books, this is a public thing made for men
to stare at; and, while doubt and failure are in mind,
mention should be made of the attempt to say something of speculative interest about thought and language, something that sprang out of Wordsworth's
poetry and his scattered reflections upon poetry. When
he was confronted with the vulgar eighteenth-century

[1] *P.W.*, Vol. III. p. 408.

definition of language as the clothing of thought, Wordsworth replied that language is not thought's dress but its incarnation.[1] His more specific remarks about language are nearly always consistent with this statement of general principle, as, for example, his protest against the Augustan element in Byron's poetry:

> the sentiment by being expressed in an *antithetical* manner, is taken out of the Region of high and imaginative feeling, to be placed in that of point and epigram. To illustrate my meaning and for no other purpose I refer to my own Lines on the Wye [*Tintern Abbey*], where you will find the same sentiment not formally put as it is here, but ejaculated as it were fortuitously in the musical succession of preconceived feeling.[2]

Wordsworth rejects the notion that poets, or other men, think a thought and then look for an attractive way of presenting it. Language is not like that. What, then, of the distinction between knowing what you think and knowing how to say it? Implicit in his remarks about language, and especially in his reckless commendations of spontaneous utterance, is the will to free the activity of thinking from association with the concept thought. The abstract question is for men like Coleridge: he is concerned in a practical way, as an empirical psychologist, with an activity which is certainly polymorphous—he would not have denied musical or mathematical thinking—but which in one of its forms is linguistic; and his knowledge of this kind does not tally with conventional descriptions.

He dislikes the dress metaphor because it suggests that language is independent of other things in a way that is untrue. It goes wrong at the start by implying that there are naked thoughts. However importunate the hubbub of life below the level of expression, only

---

[1] Reported by De Quincey, Essay on Style, *Works*, Vol. X.
[2] *Letters*, 1811-20 (ed. de Selincourt), p. 790.

error can result from talking of thoughts arising, like
Venus, from the sea of brute experience; for the false
dichotomy of thought and word is immediately encouraged. This is partly a matter of chronology, of
Wordsworth's testifying, as other artists have done,
that although you cannot start work until you know
what you want to do, it is equally the case that you do
not know what you want to do until you have done it:
so the thought has no priority in time. But more
important is his objection to the analogy of the body
and its dress. Even if Venus-Thoughts were described
as emerging fully clothed, he would still have been un-
satisfied. You can do what you like with clothes, tell
any story you please, and if language is a kind of
clothing, all use of language is a playing with words.

As always, Wordsworth's ultimate problem is a
moral and aesthetic complex. Language is moral
because of the way in which it is bound to life: it is
poetic for the same reason. His quarrel with the dress
metaphor affords an introduction to this complex since
the status of language is endangered in both connexions when it is associated with adornment or even
with working clothes. A moral-poetic responsibility is
evaded by those who think of something ready made,
waiting to be assumed. And so he challenged the
divorce of language and life, the whole idea of poetic
diction, the principles involved in Gray's famous statement that there is one language for art and another for
nature. He believed in a single language, no further
from the living heart of things than the breath that
bears it.

> For the tired slave, Song lifts the languid oar,
> And bids it aptly fall:

the Sound Ode refuses to treat language as accessory to
action: it is one of action's modes, and perhaps the
most effective. The song that lifts the oar will also, in

his own poetry, "deal boldly with substantial things":
he speaks of "the intellectual power" that

> through words and things,
> Went sounding on, a dim and perilous way.[1]

Language is in the world, pushing and being pushed
against.

When he criticizes Byron's poetry for inhabiting the
region of point and epigram, having forsaken that of
imaginative feeling, Wordsworth is protesting against
a retirement from the world, encouraged by the dress
metaphor, which makes language unable to deal boldly
with things. Projected as the conceptual currency of
men, language becomes an abstract structure, impotent
because of its isolation, the external instrument of
analytic intelligence by means of which, the Lyrical
Ballad maintains, "we murder to dissect". How can
language be more than this? In his use of the incarnation metaphor Wordsworth strikes an attitude. There
is here no contrast of living and inorganic natures, or
of enduring form and its chance habit. Above all, there
is nothing to be made and mended, no independent
construction to be managed. The dress metaphor will
not do. Nor will that variation of the dress metaphor in
which we suppose our thoughts to be shrouded in a
diaphanous linguistic film. This is to reduce language
in a different way, by ignoring it. Wordsworth's own
solution is to abandon the idea of structure for that of
function, and in his poetry to embark on the activity of
language.

I once believed that this poetry held a lesson for the
modern philosophy of linguistic analysis. In Wordsworth's solitude and relationship and in the features of
his landscape there is a conspiracy of inner and outer
which might properly be called philosophical: one may
find a public context for this private effort in the tradi-

---

[1] *The Excursion*, Bk. III. 700.

tions of western thinking, and especially in the Cartesian dichotomy of thing and thought. Confidence in the relational power of language inspires his attempt, not to deny this dichotomy, but to make it metaphysically tolerable; while an extreme sensitiveness to the logical limits of language has led philosophy in this generation to turn its back on the possibility of metaphysics. But now, when the excitement that attends beginnings has died away, it seems to me that Wordsworth has nothing to teach modern philosophers which can be turned by them to philosophical advantage. Many of them take no pleasure in the estrangement of philosophy and wisdom, do not suppose that language is a symbolic structure, abstract and determined like that of mathematics, or even wish that it were so. But the logical distress is real: within the terms of a cognitive discipline there is very little they can find to say.

It is true that Wordsworth places over against the discursive intellect a higher and still rational faculty which he calls

> clearest insight, amplitude of mind,
> And reason in her most exalted mood:[1]

and in this thrusting beyond the logic of the understanding there is a genuine metaphysical passion, a thing tougher in its mental stuff than any cult of poetic sensibility. But this is not coincident with the profession of philosophy, and does not entitle us to throw him to very professional lions. With regard to his poetry of the supernatural, I think it would be misleading to speak of philosophy at all. Not that there is anything unclear about the visions which "appeared in presence of the spiritual eye": but visions are visions, whereas the early work is of a quite different order. Here I wish to have it both ways: to claim enough of system to justify the title of Philosopher-Poet first given him by Coleridge,

[1] *The Prelude*, Bk. XIII. 169.

o

and also to avoid any joining issue with contemporary thought, even though this has become in one sense a matter of language, of which Wordsworth had a larger knowledge than philosophers.

His attitude to language is consistent with the systematic whole which I have called solitude and relationship. Language serves the principle of action and reaction, of sympathy or reciprocity, through participation. Hence his curious theory of the imagination as a conferring or abstracting of properties so that the object may itself "react upon the mind";[1] and hence the personal ambition to celebrate the mind's marriage to the world, to

> chant, in lonely peace, the spousal verse
> Of this great consummation:—and, by words
> That speak of nothing more than what we are,
> Would I arouse the sensual from their sleep
> Of Death. . . .[2]

The poet is more than chronicler or commentator because his language is woven into the texture of this process, as a function of it, and not in the ordinary sense as a description. Reality and language are a going concern.

The linguistic activity is therefore central, and at the same time there is no problem of language, no *thing* about which to be perplexed. "Where meditation was," from *The Pedlar*, is one of Wordsworth's concretized abstractions; and this Roman secret is the whole secret. Wordsworth saw the world with a systematic eccentricity due to his being born out of time in attitude to mental and physical. This means, in respect of language, an instinctive grasp of history: he is no more concerned about the difference between language and not-language than the baby who uses his voice as the most effective way of procuring the presence of his

[1] See pp. 44-5.   [2] Preface to *The Excursion*.

mother. The infancy of the race may have been a little like that—the remote ancestor of the poet who wished to deal boldly with things.

Born into time, Wordsworth said that language is the incarnation of thought. Thought incarnate is not thought expressed, or there would be no need to distinguish the word and the mathematical symbol; but when he refuses to allow that thoughts are clothed in words, he fears not so much a direct confusion with mathematics as the reducing of language to a conceptual instrument, external to those who use it. Language must have a corresponding inwardness in order to enact the reciprocity of nature.

We begin, then, with the concretized abstractions: with the River Duddon which has

> No meaner Poet than the whistling Blast,
> And Desolation is thy Patron-saint;

and Toussaint L'Ouverture, imprisoned for defying Napoleon:

> There's not a breathing of the common wind
> That will forget thee; thou hast great allies;
> Thy friends are exultations, agonies,
> And love. . . .

In both cases the abstract nouns are associated with the action of the wind, which in its double movement is the most important feature of the Wordsworthian landscape. This is what they mean.

Four-syllable abstract nouns in "-ion" are very common in Wordsworth's poetry, and usually, as here with "exultations", they occupy the fourth to the seventh syllables of the decasyllabic line. *Tintern Abbey*, the supreme example of his blank-verse prosody, has three, all in this position. "Visitation", an important word in *The Prelude*, of the same kind as "Presence" and "Power", appears three times in the 1805 version of Book I, and on each occasion it holds the middle of the line, immense, bare, a windlike echoing. Wordsworth often uses these nouns at a decisive point in his argument. This is true of

> the spousal verse
> Of this great consummation

which we have just noticed, and of the "authentic tidings" of

> central peace, subsisting at the heart
> Of endless agitation

with which he concludes the account of the child listening to the shell in *The Excursion*. For this and for other reasons, Arnold should not have said that Wordsworth has no style.

The famous sonnet that begins:

> It is a beauteous evening, calm and free,
> The holy time is quiet as a Nun
> Breathless with adoration; . . .

betrays his authorship in several ways. "Adoration" is one sign. The simile is another, and the strange unviolence in which it relates very different natures, the woman and the hour. "Holy" is certainly a kind of bond between them, but the essence of the thing is his unselfconscious movement from abstract to concrete. In his Westminster Bridge sonnet he says that the city

> doth, like a garment, wear
> The beauty of the morning. . . .

To this a friend objected that he goes on to describe the city as "silent, bare", thus contradicting himself. Wordsworth admitted this fault, and in a letter he altered the sonnet so as to omit the garment image.[1]

---

[1] *Letters*, 1831-40 (ed. de Selincourt), p. 812.

But the alteration was never adopted. He felt that the image was necessary, and we can see why:

> Earth has not anything to show more fair:
> Dull would he be of soul who could pass by
> A sight so touching in its majesty:
> This City now doth, like a garment, wear
> The beauty of the morning; silent, bare. . . .

It is needed to sustain, strengthen, and illuminate the "sight so touching in its majesty". The weak physical metaphor of "touching" gains sudden pathetic force through this association; and in the balancing of "touching . . . majesty" with "garment . . . beauty" the poem's nature is confirmed.

"Breathless", too, from the Holy Time sonnet, is characteristic of Wordsworth. There is unexpected tension and effort in the shift of stress to the first syllable, and the situation of the word allows its silent concentration to flood back through the line end pause. He makes a similar, though more obvious use of this pause in *The Prelude* account of the boy who hooted to the owls and then waited for them to answer him:

> Then sometimes, in that silence, while he hung
> Listening. . . .[1]

Language takes time—time backwards as well as time forwards.

This poet of many short words has a very careful use of the single long word. The best of the Ecclesiastical Sonnets compares the outward forms of truth with a ruined tower,

>   which royally did wear
> Her crown of weeds, but could not even sustain
> Some casual shout that broke the silent air,
> Or the unimaginable touch of Time.[2]

---

[1] Bk. V. 406.   [2] *Mutability*.

One of his many lonely women wonders what has become of her son: [Perhaps thou]

> hast been summoned to the deep,
> Thou, and all thy mates, to keep
> An incommunicable sleep.[1]

When he stole game from another boy's snare, Wordsworth heard, following him,

> sounds
> Of undistinguishable motion, steps
> Almost as silent as the turf they trod.[2]

In *Tintern Abbey* he speaks of the state

> In which the heavy and the weary weight
> Of all this unintelligible world
> Is lightened. . . .

All these words arrest the movement of the sense which is usually easy and swift, though in the last example laboriously slow; and while they are going on they give the means of new awareness through release from the poem's time scale. The murmured succession, the fearful patter, the prolonged striving, are different kinds of escape almost from language itself, to experience-worlds outside language.

These words are united in their negative form as well as in their length. Wordsworth carries his delight in negatives to the point of tiresome mannerism: there are too many double negatives, such as "not unnoticed"; too much rhetorical piling of adjective on adjective—"unchastened, unsubdued, unawed, unraised"—and pointless circumlocution—"not seldom" and "nor seldom" appear five times in the final text of *The Prelude*. But the roots of this practice run very deep: the balance of positive and negative is a mode of reciprocity, like echo and reflection in his landscape. It also

---

[1] *The Affliction of Margaret.*   [2] *The Prelude*, Bk. I. 330.

shows the unmathematical nature of language. If two
minuses make a plus, it is a special kind of plus: the
negative form can be on its own account heart-piercing.

> Six weeks beneath the moving sea
> He lay in slumber quietly;
> Unforced by wind or wave
> To quit the Ship for which he died. . . .[1]

Wordsworth believed that the problem of thought
issuing into language had been considered too much in
isolation, at the expense of language's impingement
upon the very mentality of mind. In this he felt no
logical embarrassment: the double movement was as
evident to him as the principle of sympathy in nature,
was in fact an aspect of that principle. We saw how, in
The Borderers, a star once held a man from murder.
Words have their corresponding authority; and it is
the moral-poetic duty of all who use them to command
attention of the precise quality required, and to command it for true ends. Sometimes language will fail:
here, as with Nature's unrequited love for Peter Bell,
Wordsworth's optimism was always precarious.

The poet's command of attention has often been
spoken of as an incantatory skill. This is peculiarly ill-
suited to Wordsworth's matter of fact and his reliance
on daylight powers. Nor is the idea of controlled
ambiguity in poetic statement much more serviceable;
for it must not imply, in his case, intellectual deliberation. Nor is the thing experienced as ambiguity. In *The
Prelude* he speaks of

> heights
> Clothed in the sunshine of the withering fern.[2]

This, the 1850 and final text, has no less than five fore-
runners.[3] The 1805 text speaks simply of "the moun-

---

[1] *Sweet Flower! belike . . .*   [2] 1850, Bk. VI. 10.
[3] *Wordsworth's "Prelude"* (ed. de Selincourt), pp. 170-1.

tain pomp of Autumn", which is later expanded by
reference to the colour of the hills under autumn sun:

> the beauty and pomp
> Of Autumn, entering under azure skies
> To mountains clothed in yellow robe of fire.

He may have had the colour of the vegetation in mind,
as well as that of the sunlight, but he has not yet
succeeded in saying so. In the fourth version he gives
up the attempt to mention colour, and returns in effect
to 1805. The "golden fern" appears in his fifth version,
which paves the way for the final confluence of sun and
vegetation. Autumn is not mentioned because the
season is already known from the context.

"Clothed in sunshine" is easy: so is "clothed in the
withering fern". But "clothed in the sunshine of the
withering fern" is odd, its oddness resting in "of", and
the different kinds of work it has to do. One might say
that the word is ambiguous; but this would be a perverse way of expressing it, since the block-impression
of the phrase is clear, even without knowing its history.
We admit "of" as we admit others of Wordsworth's
busy prepositions: in their degree they are the stride
of his thought.

"Every great and original writer, in proportion as he
is great or original, must himself . . . teach the art by
which he is to be seen."[1] I have applied Wordsworth's
general rule to his own poetry, in the hope of showing
a *fait accompli;* the art well taught, the attention commanded. This is an achievement shared by the concretized abstractions, the mental-physical imagery, the
captive labours of the verb "to be"; by the short
words, the long words, and all the time and space of
language. Shared, too, by language's humblest parts.
"And", more frequent in Wordsworth than in any
poet, is the preserver of extreme structural simplicity

---

[1] *Letters,* 1806-11, x. (ed. de Selincourt), p. 130.

through hundreds of lines of *Prelude* narrative: if the ice is thin, the skating is light and swift. "And" helps to sustain the calm elevation of *Tintern Abbey:*

> And the round ocean and the living air,
> And the blue sky, and in the mind of man. . . .

By its monotony, its insistence on the particular, "and" develops Wordsworth's expository style, in common with other words of modest function—"but", "thus", "therefore". Notice, in *Tintern Abbey*, how the two cadences:

> Therefore am I still
> A lover of the meadows

and

> Therefore let the moon
> Shine on thee:

introduce a logical, knitted quality; cause the reader to glance behind and collect the poem for himself.

"Therefore" is a confidence trick and "of" an ambiguity only if Wordsworth's view of language is rejected for one more congenial because less fateful. Otherwise, following him to "the great Nature that exists in works Of mighty Poets", we can share what seems to be a divine joke—that this poet should bear the name he does.

INDEX OF PERSONS

INDEX OF WORDSWORTH'S POEMS